COOK \
MW01672835

IDEAS FOR TEACHERS

COOK WITH ME

Language development through cooking activities, poems, and stories

by Lorelei Liddelow

PEGUIS PUBLISHERS

520 Hargrave Street, Winnipeg, Manitoba, Canada R3A 0X8

First published 1989
by Longman and Cheshire Ltd.,
Melbourne, Australia

Illustrated by Ian Forss

Canadian Cataloguing in Publication Data

Liddelow, Lorelei
Cook with me

(Ideas for teachers)
ISBN 0-920541-95-X

1. Language arts (Primary). 2. Language arts (Preschool). 3. Cookery.
4. Creative activities and seat work. I. Forss, Ian. II. Title. III. Series.
LB1528.L532 1990 372.6'044 C90-097040-5

Acknowledgment
The publishers would like to thank the principal, staff, and children of Chancellor School (Winnipeg) for their cooperation in the preparation of the cover of this book.

Printed and bound in Canada.

Contents

About this book

Cook With Me continues the author's approach to language development in the classroom found in *Talk With Me* and *Fly With Me*, the other books in this series.

This third book has a special focus on foods, nutrition, and classroom cooking activities with stories, poems, plays, and other language activities included to enrich the children's experience in each session. The plays may be photocopied for classroom use.

The recipes for each cooking activity are simple for children to follow and ingredients are readily available. The associated language activities are also centered on topics which teachers usually wish to include in their program for the school year.

Cook With Care

We know how
To cook with care
So germs and flies
And bugs...beware!
Of kitchen dangers
We're aware
We know how
To cook with care!

WANTED!

BERTIE GERM

Bertie Germ
Ran away
From the garbage dump
One day.
Where will he go?
What will he do?
Will he come
And live with YOU?

Cook With Care

STORYMAKING

1. Teacher distributes the posters (copies of page 2), reads the rhyme, and tells the beginning of the story:

   Bertie Germ was bored with living in the garbage dump so one day he hitched a ride on a garbage truck and...

2. Through questioning, the teacher guides the children to create a story plot. For example,

   BEGINNING: Where was Bertie when he got off the truck?
   What sort of a place was it?
   Who lived there?
   What happened when Bertie met them?

   MIDDLE: How did Bertie feel?
   So what did he do?
   Was Bertie in more trouble?
   Who else came along?
   What did they say?
   What happened next?

   END: What happened to them all?
   How did the story end?
   How did Bertie feel then?

3. Teacher may need to retell the story, weaving the children's ideas into a story line. Most young children, however, should be able to retell the story without prompting.
4. After several "whole-class" stories have been created, small-group "storymaking" could be introduced.
5. Stories could be recorded and illustrated by the children as class or individual storybooks.

PICTURE TALK (USING THE KITCHEN PICTURE)

1. During the recess prior to a cooking session, teacher prepares and conceals:
   - soap, towel
   - a bowl of water
   - comb, brush
   - nail file, nailbrush
   - a clean apron
2. Teacher arranges to have a colleague supervise children's return from recess.

3. Teacher transforms his/her appearance:
   - smudges on face
   - dirty hands and fingernails
   - dishevelled hair
   - undone buttons, belts, sleeves, shoelaces
4. When children are settled, teacher makes an entrance, waits for a reaction!
5. If met with silence (most unlikely!) teacher asks: "Should I be allowed to cook in this dirty state? What shall I do?"
6. Toiletries are revealed and teacher restores appearance.
7. Children discuss clean cooking habits, especially cleaning-up-after-cooking activities.
8. Teacher asks: "What sort of cooking places does Bertie Germ *love* to visit?"
   - dirty hands
   - dirty fingernails
   - grubby dish towels
   - stained aprons
   - sloppy spills
   - grimy tables and counter tops
   - uncovered food (on utensils, stoves, floors, and in garbage cans, bowls, and saucepans)
   - greasy sinks
   - smelly drains
   - mooshy, mucky, messy piles of unwashed dishes!
9. Teacher distributes copies of the kitchen picture (page 4). Children observe.
10. Teacher asks: "Where has Bertie Germ been in this kitchen picture?"
11. Children discuss and illustrate the picture with their versions of *Bertie Germ footprints*.

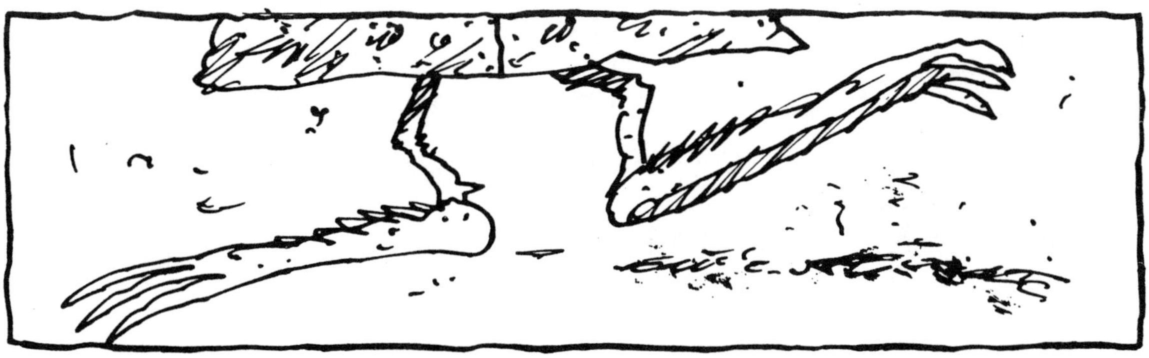

GIVING DIRECTIONS FOR SAFE COOKING

Signs We Know

Signs we know
Signs we know
STOP and *GO*
Are signs we know
STOP and *GO*
STOP and *GO*
STOP and *GO*
Are signs we know.

1. Teacher reads the poem (above) and guides the conversation. Children talk about safety:
   - traffic signs
   - traffic lights
   - crosswalks
   - road safety rules

2. Teacher extends the subject matter to include safe cooking signs and rules. Children devise rules:

SIGNS — Learn to read:

ON	OFF
HOT	COLD
OPEN	CLOSED

BURNS	Take care with hot water, cooking fat, oil, steam, hot surfaces, hot utensils and pot handles.
CLOTHING	Use oven mitts or potholders.
CUTS	Handle knives, peelers, graters, openers, scissors, and skewers with care.
FALLS	Mop up food spills on floors.
COLLISIONS	Turn protruding pot and pan handles away from walk-through areas. Don't leave cords dangling. Avoid leaving cupboard doors and drawers open.

We-Are-What-We-Eat

Decide what healthy foods
To cook
Then look them up
In your recipe book!

Fruits Are Healthy Foods

RECIPE: ***Fruit Kebabs***

INGREDIENTS:
apples
oranges
bananas

UTENSILS:
knives
wooden skewers

METHOD:
1. wash apples
2. peel oranges and bananas
3. chop fruit into chunks
4. thread fruit chunks onto wooden skewers

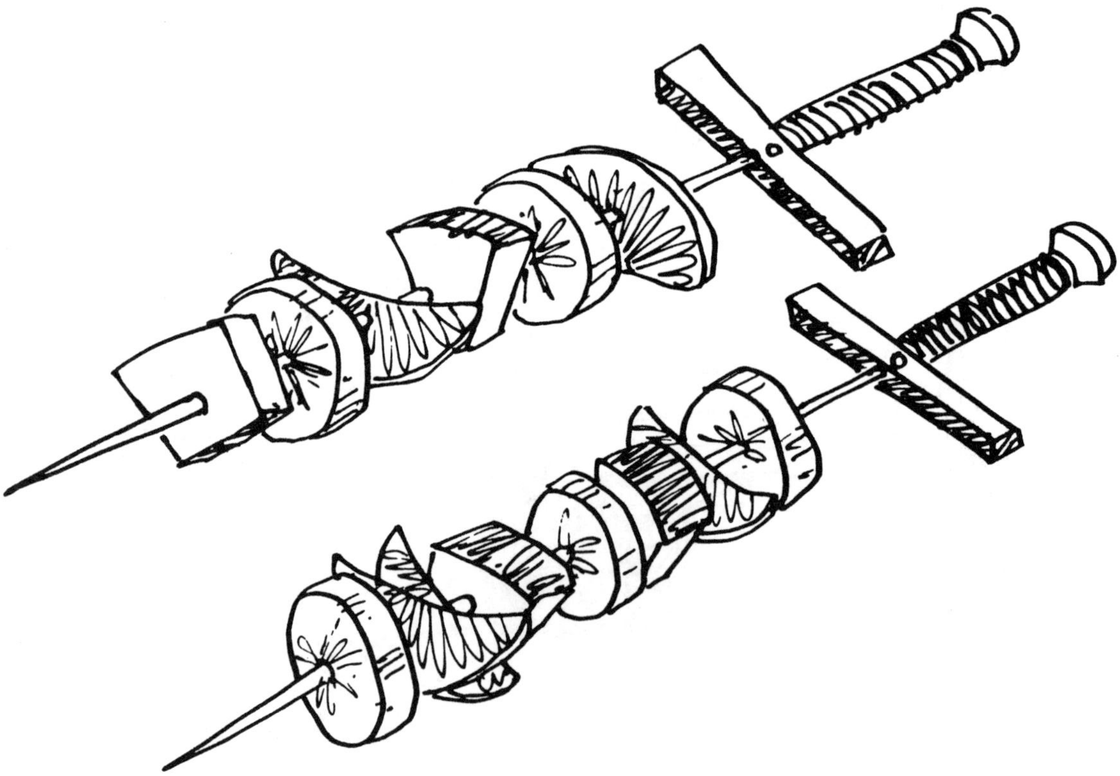

Juicy Fruits

Crunchy munchy apples
Squishy squashy plums
Squirty spurty oranges
Yum! Yum! Yum!

A TASTE TABLE

1. Display varieties of the same fruit.
   Children taste and tell.
   For example, **apples**—*Granny Smith, McIntosh, Delicious.*
2. Provide fresh and processed examples of a fruit.
   Children taste and tell.
   For example, **apricots**—fresh, cooked, canned, dried, in jam.

A Taste Test

Here's a test
For you to do
Do these taste
The same to you?

A TASTE MOBILE

1. Suspend fruits from a mobile, improvised from a coat hanger and thread.
   Let children choose a fruit, then taste and tell.
   For example, **Citrus fruits**—segments of orange, lemon, grapefruit
   Stone fruits—peach, plum, nectarine pieces.
   Dried fruits—currants, raisins, figs, dates, apricots.

STORYTELLING

William Tell

an apple story

Many years ago in a beautiful country of mountains, lakes, and forests there lived a brave man called William Tell. William Tell and his neighbors were fine, hardworking people, but they were also very unhappy. A cruel tyrant called Gessler ruled over them. Gessler, who lived in a great, dark castle and who kept many soldiers, demanded that the people give him most of the fish they caught in the lakes and the crops they grew in their fields.

The people were too frightened to do anything else. Gessler tormented them beyond endurance. He even had his hat placed on a pole in the marketplace and his soldiers forced the people to bow to the hat. Everyone obeyed without question. Everyone, that is, except William Tell.

William refused to bow before the hat and just as the soldiers seized him, Gessler himself arrived at the marketplace. He had heard of William Tell, who was known to have much skill with the bow and arrow.

"We shall see who is master here," said Gessler. "Fetch William Tell's son."

The frightened crowd trembled as the soldiers dragged the boy forward.

"Place an apple on his head," ordered Gessler. "You must shoot the apple off the head of your son," he told William Tell. "If you succeed, you may go free. If you miss, I shall have you killed."

The boy looked into his father's eyes. The love he saw there made him feel brave, and he

forced himself to stand straight and very still.

William Tell drew two arrows from his quiver. He slipped one arrow inside his doublet. The other arrow he fitted to his bow. He took aim, drew the bow, and the first arrow flew through the air and pierced the apple. The crowd wept with joy as William Tell clasped his son in his arms.

Gessler was furious.

"Why did you choose two arrows?" he demanded.

"If I had killed my son my second arrow would have been for you, Gessler," replied William Tell.

"Seize him!" roared Gessler.

The soldiers threw William Tell into Gessler's boat to take him across the lake to Gessler's castle.

But William Tell was in luck. A fierce storm arose and the soldiers could not steer the boat in the wild waves. William Tell was a fine oarsman and he brought the boat safely to shore. As it reached the bank he leaped onto land and escaped deep into the forest. Around him gathered his friends and neighbors. The time had come to rise up against the tyrant, Gessler.

William Tell and his men hid in the woods outside the castle and as Gessler and his soldiers approached, William Tell drew his bow and Gessler fell to the ground—an arrow through his heart.

Gessler's soldiers fled, never to return, and after that day the people were free. Their country, known today as Switzerland, prospered in peace.

Vegetables Are Healthy Foods

A Salad Song

(To the tune *I'm a Little Teapot*)

I'm a little salad
Made of greens
Radishes, tomatoes
Celery and beans
Crunchy, crunchy carrots
Lettuce, peas
Serve me fresh
And eat me please.

RECIPE: ***Friendship Salad***

1. Teacher and children arrange a "vegetable walk" through the produce section in the supermarket.
2. Each child brings fifty cents from home to purchase a salad vegetable.
3. Teacher provides children with individual shopping lists.

4. Children return to school and prepare the *Friendship Salad.*
5. They wash, peel, chop vegetables and combine them on a large platter.

Bread and Cereals Are Healthy Foods

RECIPE: ***Biscuits***

INGREDIENTS:

1 cup whole wheat flour (250 ml)
1 cup all purpose flour (250 ml)
½ teaspoon salt (2 ml)
1 teaspoon sugar (5 ml)
⅓ cup butter/margarine (75 ml)
¾ cup milk (175 ml)
3 teaspoons baking powder (15 ml)

UTENSILS:

sieve or sifter
mixing bowl
set of measuring spoons
measuring cups
rolling pin
1 glass jar (3" diameter) or biscuit cutter
baking pan
pastry blender or fork

METHOD:
1. sift flour and salt into the bowl
2. stir in sugar and baking powder
3. cut in butter margarine until crumbly
4. add milk slowly—mix to soft dough
5. on a floured surface, roll dough to 2.5 cm thickness
6. cut with top of floured glass or cutter and place on an ungreased cookie sheet
7. bake at 450°F (250°C) 12–15 minutes

Little Red Hen

(a poem about bread)

CHORUS: Little Red Hen
Went out one day
She found some wheat
Along the way.

LITTLE RED HEN: "Who will plant
This wheat?" she said.

CHORUS: But all her friends
Just shook their heads.

DUCK: "Not I," said the Duck.

CAT: "Not I," said the Cat.

DOG: "Not I," said the Dog.

CHORUS: "Fancy that!"

LITTLE RED HEN: "Then I will plant
This wheat," she said.

DUCK, CAT, DOG: "And we will all
Go back to bed."

CHORUS: Little Red Hen
Went out one day
To cut some wheat
Along the way.

LITTLE RED HEN: "Who will cut
This wheat?" she said.

CHORUS: But all her friends
Just shook their heads.

DUCK: "Not I," said the Duck.

CAT: "Not I," said the Cat.

DOG: "Not I," said the Dog.

CHORUS: "Fancy that!"

LITTLE RED HEN: "Then I will cut
This wheat," she said.

DUCK, CAT, DOG: "And we will all
Go back to bed."

CHORUS: Little Red Hen
Went out one day
To thresh the wheat
Along the way.

LITTLE RED HEN: "Who will thresh
This wheat," she said.

CHORUS: But all her friends
Just shook their heads.

DUCK: "Not I," said the Duck.

CAT: "Not I," said the Cat.

DOG: "Not I," said the Dog.

CHORUS: "Fancy that!"

LITTLE RED HEN: "Then I will thresh
This wheat," she said.

DUCK, CAT, DOG: "And we will all
Go back to bed."

* * * * * *

CHORUS: Little Red Hen
Went out one day
To grind the wheat
Along the way.

LITTLE RED HEN: "Who will grind
This wheat?" she said.

DUCK: "Not I," said the Duck.

CAT: "Not I," said the Cat.

DOG: "Not I," said the Dog.

CHORUS: "Fancy that!"

LITTLE RED HEN: "Then I will grind
This wheat," she said.

DUCK, CAT, DOG: "And we will all
Go back to bed."

* * * * * *

CHORUS: Little Red Hen
Went out one day
To bake some bread
Along the way.

LITTLE RED HEN: "Who will bake
This bread?" she said.

CHORUS: But all her friends
Just shook their heads.

DUCK: "Not I," said the Duck.

CAT: "Not I," said the Cat.

DOG: "Not I," said the Dog.

CHORUS: "Fancy that!"

LITTLE RED HEN: "Then I will bake
This bread," she said.

DUCK, CAT, DOG: "And we will all
Go back to bed."

* * * * * *

CHORUS: Little Red Hen
Went out one day
To eat the bread
Along the way.

LITTLE RED HEN: "Who will eat
This bread?" she said.

CHORUS: Her friends began
To nod their heads.

DUCK: "I will!" said the Duck.

CAT: "I will!" said the Cat.

DOG: "I will!" said the Dog.

CHORUS: "Fancy that!"

LITTLE RED HEN: "No, I will eat
This bread," she said.

ALL: *And she did!*

* * * * * *

Meat, Fish, Chicken, and Eggs Are Healthy Foods

RECIPE: ***Tunaburgers***

INGREDIENTS:

3 potatoes
2 teaspoons butter (10 ml)
1 small onion
1 7 oz. can of tuna (196 g)
1 Tbsp. parsley (15 ml)
½ cup seasoned flour (125 ml)
2 eggs
½ cup breadcrumbs (125 ml)
margarine or oil for cooking

UTENSILS:

peeler
knife
saucepan
set of measuring spoons
grater
fork or potato masher
2 large plates for flour, and crumbs
1 bowl for beating eggs
1 whisk
1 frying pan
1 spatula

METHOD:

1. peel and boil potatoes
2. grate onion while potatoes are cooking
3. chop parsley
4. drain tuna
5. mash potatoes with butter
6. mix potatoes, onion, parsley, tuna
7. form mixture into tunaburgers
8. coat with seasoned flour
9. beat eggs, dip tunaburgers
10. coat in breadcrumbs
11. cook in frying pan until golden brown

The Magic Fish

(a fishy tale)

There was once a fisherman
And his wife
Who led a most
Unhappy life.
They were hungry and cold
And wretched and poor
And they lived in a hut
By the wild seashore.

As the fisherman pulled
In his nets one day
He heard a voice
Beside him say.
"Listen to me
I'm a magic fish
And you may have
A magic wish."

"Just let me loose
And set me free
And throw me back
Into the sea."
The fisherman did
As he was told
But his wife when she heard
Began to scold.

"What a fool you were
Not to make a wish
Go back at once
To the magic fish.
This hut is a hovel,
A pigsty," she said
"Tell him I want
A cottage instead."

The fish just smiled
"The spell has begun
Return to your wife
The deed is done."
And the fisherman found
To his great surprise
A cottage stood
Before his eyes.

"How cozy it is,"
The fisherman thought
But his greedy wife
Began to find fault.
"This place is too pokey
And small," she said
"Tell him I want
A mansion instead."

"But Wife," said her husband
"That's quite absurd
It's the silliest thing
I've ever heard."
But she wept and wailed
'Til he went to the fish
"My wife," he said
"Has changed her wish."

The fish just nodded
"The spell has begun
Return to your wife
The deed is done."
And sure enough
Where the cottage had been
Stood the grandest house
He'd ever seen.

At first his wife
Was full of joy
But she soon grew tired
Of her fine new toy.
Her newfound riches
Had gone to her head
"This time I want
A *palace*," she said.

"No, wife," said her husband
"Indeed you do not
Be grateful instead
For the house you've got."
But her ranting and raving
Filled the air
And drove the poor man
To despair.

And full of shame
To the fish he fled
"I'm afraid she's changed
Her wish," he said.
This time the fish frowned
"The spell has begun
Return to your wife
The deed is done."

Then the magic fish
Swam away from the shore
Far out to sea
And was seen no more
And the fisherman wept
For well he knew
What he'd find at home
I know...do *you*?

DISCUSSION

1. Teacher reads the poem.
   - What do you think the fisherman found at home?
   - Why did the characters act the way they did?

   Children consider the mood of the poem:
   - Did you feel sorry for the fisherman's wife? Why? Why not?
   - If you had been the Magic Fish how would you have felt when the wife kept wanting him to grant her more wishes?
   - What sort of person was the fisherman?

2. Teacher relates the subject matter to the children's experiences.

   Children consider whether or not people should have all they want:
   - If you caught a Magic Fish what would you wish for?
   - What did you wish for last Christmas?
   - Did you receive everything you asked for?
   - Why do you think you can (or cannot) have all the things you want?

3. Teacher extends the subject matter to develop in the children a positive attitude towards eating nutritious foods.

   Teacher asks:
   - Have you ever caught a fish? What happened?
   - Have you ever cooked a fish? How did it taste?

   Tell your neighbor all about it.

Milk and Milk Foods Are Healthy Foods

RECIPE: ***Yogurt Surprise***

INGREDIENTS:
1 cup plain yogurt (250 ml)
1 orange
2 Tbsp. honey (30 ml)

UTENSILS:
1 mixing bowl
set of measuring spoons
1 juice squeezer
1 grater

METHOD:
1. pour yogurt into bowl
2. squeeze orange with juicer
3. pour three tablespoons of juice into bowl—stir
4. grate rind of orange finely
5. add grated rind to dip—stir
6. add honey and mix well
7. serve with fresh fruit at recess

The Billy Goats Gruff

(a milk-food poem 'cause goats eat grass to make milk)

"Enough is enough"
Cried the Billy Goats Gruff
"We've had nothing to eat
All day.
Across the river
Grows fresh green grass
And it's only a bridge away."

Little Goat Gruff
Was made of tough stuff
"I'll cross the bridge first,"
Said he.
"A bad bold Troll
Lives under the bridge
But the Troll won't frighten me!"

But his trippy-trip-trap
Woke the Troll from his nap
"I'm coming to eat you!"
He roared.
"Oh don't eat me
Wait for Middle Goat Gruff,"
Little Goat Gruff implored.

Middle Goat Gruff
Was made of rough stuff
"I'll cross the bridge next,"
Said he.
"A bad bold Troll
Lives under the bridge
But the Troll won't frighten me!"

But his trippy-trip-trap
Woke the Troll from his nap,
"I'm coming to eat you!"
He roared.
"Oh, don't eat me
Wait for Great Goat Gruff,"
Middle Goat Gruff implored.

Great Goat Gruff
Was made of gruff stuff
"I'll cross the bridge last,"
Said he.
"A bad bold Troll
Lives under the bridge
But the Troll won't frighten me!"

But his trippy-trip-trap
Woke the Troll from his nap
"I'm coming to eat you!"
He roared.
"Coming to eat me!"
Roared Great Goat Gruff
"Delighted to have you aboard!"

The Troll was as tough
And as rough and as gruff
And a terrible fight
Took place,
'Til Great Goat Gruff
Tossed him over the bridge
And he sank like a stone
Without trace.

Now the Billy Goats Gruff
Eat their green grassy stuff
At peace on the river bank there,
But the message is clear
To all Trolls living near
This is Goat Country now
So BEWARE!

A Troll Riddle

(for teachers only?)

Why was the Troll
So bad and bold?

Because the Troll
Had a hole in his soul.

Teacher asks:
- Where does milk come from?
- What milk foods do we eat or drink?

STORYMAKING

The Town Mouse and the Country Mouse

(cheese is a milk food)

Once upon a time a Country Mouse invited his cousin, a Town Mouse, to stay.

The Country Mouse lived under a hedge in a snug, cozy nest of straw.

He led a quiet but happy life.

When the Town Mouse arrived, his country cousin made him very welcome and they sat down to a simple meal of bread and cheese.

The Town Mouse nibbled politely at a morsel of cheese and swallowed a few crumbs of bread.

"I usually take a little stroll through the meadow after dinner," said the Country Mouse as he poured his cousin an acorn cup of fresh water.

"How exciting for you," thought the Town Mouse. He was not impressed with country life.

He took a few sips of water then he said, "Why don't you take a little holiday, cousin, and visit me in town?"

And so it was arranged.

When the Country Mouse arrived in the big city he was amazed. Everything looked and smelt and sounded so different from the countryside he knew.

The Town Mouse showed him around the grand house where he lived.

They went into the great dining room where a delicious banquet was prepared.

The two little mice climbed on to the huge table and feasted on cookies and cakes and strawberries and wine. The food and drink were too rich for the Country Mouse and he began to feel quite ill.

Just then the great doors opened and the guests entered. The barking of the house dogs could be heard from the hall.

The two little mice fled down to the cellar where the Town Mouse lived.

The fierce kitchen cat chased them and they only just managed to escape.

"Goodbye, cousin," said the Country Mouse.

"But you've only just arrived!" cried the Town Mouse in dismay.

"Yes," agreed the Country Mouse.

"Better cheese and water
in peace
Than cakes and wine
in fear."

And with that he bade farewell to the Town Mouse and scampered as fast as he could back to the quiet, comfortable, country life that he knew.

*Children would enjoy creating further adventures of the Town Mouse and the Country Mouse.

The Tale Of Two Mice

(a romance)

Once there was a city mouse
A soft and silky pretty mouse
Who lived alone in her town house
And knew the city ways.

By chance the pretty city mouse
Met a jolly country mouse
Who'd come to town to see the sights
And have a holiday.

And so the pretty city mouse
And the jolly country mouse
Met each other every day
And danced each night away.

And as they danced, the country mouse
Told the pretty city mouse
All about his country house
And his country ways.

"Perhaps one day, dear City Mouse,"
Said the jolly country mouse,
"You'll come to see my country house."
"Perhaps," she said, "I may."

But all too soon the country mouse
Had to tell the city mouse,
"My holiday is over
I must leave for home today."

'Twas then the pretty city mouse
Knew she loved the country mouse
If only she could go with him
And leave her city ways.

Then said the jolly country mouse
"Marry me, dear City Mouse!"
"Oh yes!" she cried, so he and she
Were wed without delay.

And in their cozy country house
Now dwell the jolly country mouse
And his soft and silky city mouse
Content in every way.

RECIPE: ***Cheese Straws***

INGREDIENTS:
- 1 ½ cups all-purpose flour (375 ml)
- 1 teaspoon salt (5 ml)
- pinch of cayenne
- dash of pepper
- ½ cup cheddar cheese (125 ml)
- ¾ cup margarine (175 ml)
- 3 Tbsp. water (45 ml)

UTENSILS:
- mixing bowl
- set of measuring spoons
- measuring cups
- knife or pastry blender
- grater
- mixing spoon
- rolling pin
- greased cookie sheet

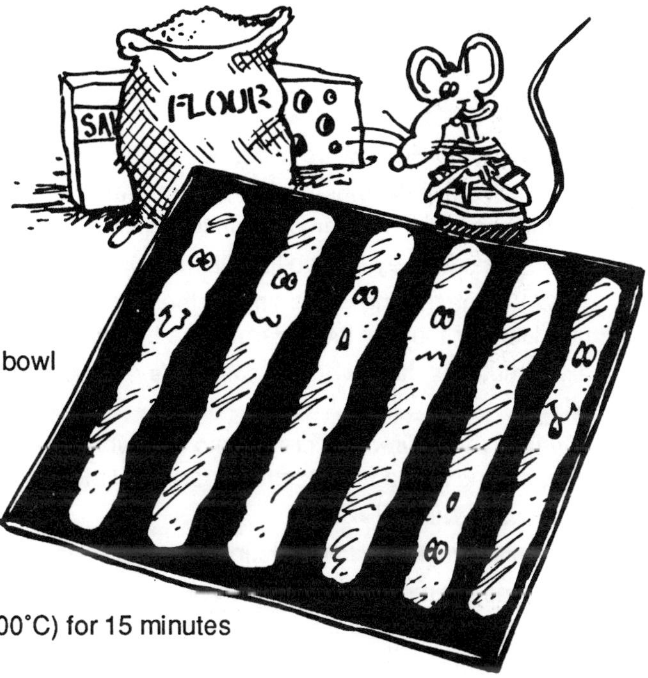

METHOD:
1. combine flour, salt, pepper, cayenne into bowl
2. cut up margarine
3. cut into flour until no lumps are left
4. grate cheese, mix into flour
5. add water to make dough
6. knead lightly
7. roll out to 0.5 centimetres thick
8. cut into strips
9. place on greased tray—bake at 400°F (200°C) for 15 minutes

Butter and Margarine Are Healthy Foods—If They're Lightly Spread!

Butter

Just a dab of butter
If it's lightly spread
Is tasty on a nice hot scone
Or healthy wholewheat
bread.

Butter Churning

Turn the cream
In the churn
Taste it with a spoon
Turn the cream
In the churn
You'll have butter soon.

Making Butter

Walter and Emily were two small children who lived on a dairy farm many years ago.

Life was hard in those days. Before they went to school and when they came home, Walter and Emily helped to get the cows in for milking.

Sometimes they helped to milk the cows, too.

When the milking was finished, their father separated the cream which would be made into butter. He sold most of the cream to the butter factory.

Sometimes, however, the children's mother put some cream aside to make butter for the family.

First, she poured the cream into a bowl. Then she stirred and stirred with a flat wooden spoon, adding a little salt as she stirred, until the cream turned into butter.

It was delicious!

Walter and Emily loved eating slices of their mother's homemade bread and butter.

But sometimes when the heavy rains came and the clover grew lush and thick in the fields, their mother's butter tasted different. It tasted strongly of clover.

Walter and Emily did not like this strong clover flavor and they would not eat the butter on their bread. But they were not usually fussy eaters. They always ate all the other tasty, nourishing food their mother set before them, so nothing was said about the butter.

Teacher asks:

- Why do you think the butter tasted of clover?
- Have you ever tasted homemade butter?

RECIPE: **_Making Butter_**
(a small-group activity)

INGREDIENTS:
1 cup very cold cream (at least 22% butterfat) (250 ml)
1 Tbsp. salt (15 ml) (or to taste)

UTENSILS:
1 glass jar with lid
1 tablespoon

METHOD:
1. place cream in glass jar
2. children take turns shaking until cream turns to butter
3. wash butter under a tap
4. press butter against the side of the jar with back of spoon
5. remove liquid when clear
6. add salt to butter
7. children taste and tell

Before-and-After

This story's sad
Without a doubt
A greedy pirate
It's about
But things get better
Later on
So turn the page
And read along!

Bad Food and Good Food

RECIPE: ***Pirate Ships***
(a small-group activity)

INGREDIENTS:
submarine rolls
butter/margarine
carrots
tomatoes
cucumbers
beef/chicken/turkey slices
Swiss cheese slices

UTENSILS:
knives
forks
peelers
graters
small wooden skewers

METHOD:
1. cut rolls in half lengthwise
2. scoop out bread filling with fork
3. butter the hollowed-out rolls using butter or margarine
4. peel and grate carrots—line rolls with grated carrot
5. peel cucumbers—slice cucumbers and tomatoes, then place slices in layers on grated carrot
6. put slices of meat on top of the slices of cucumber and tomato
7. cut cheese to simulate a ship's sails—secure with cocktail sticks or toothpicks
8. cut into serving-sized pieces and eat for lunch with pieces of fruit

Percy the Pirate

Percy was a pirate
He'd been one since a lad
And though he was quite naughty
He wasn't really bad.

Handy with a cutlass
He'd wield a bold slish-slash
And chase a cheeky villain
'Til he backed off down the hatch.

Percy wore an earring
In each dirty ear
He'd tattoos, knives, and pistols
The usual pirate gear.

His teeth had all been knocked out
In battles, brawls, and fights
And when he smiled his gummy leer
It was a dreadful sight.

He had a bald old parrot
Who talked and squawked all day
It sat on Percy's shoulder
And kept the flies away.

Percy was a greedy-guts
He really was obese
He gobbled junk food all day long
All drippy with fat and grease.

But worst of all, old Percy
Became an awful bore
His mates had heard his stories
A hundred times before.

So what with Percy's parrot
His junk food and his jokes
They planned to banish Percy
Where he wouldn't upset folks.

They packed up his belongings
His share of gold and loot
And they stuck him on an island
With some coconuts and fruit.

They gave him a new joke book
To wile away the days
And they waved "Goodbye" to Percy
And gaily sailed away.

Did Percy feel unhappy
And forlorn about it all?
"You must be joking," Percy said,
"I'm going to have a ball!"

Percy and his parrot
Quickly settled down
He threw away his junk food
And soon was trim and brown.

He made a lovely veggie patch
And built a barbecue
A little shop, some cute grass huts
And then a spa or two.

He stuck a great big notice
Upon a tall palm tree
"COME TO TREASURE ISLAND"
And signed it *Percy P.*

Tourists flocked to Percy
On every wave and tide
To visit Treasure Island
They came from far and wide.

In "Percy's Pirate Gift Shop"
He'd treasure maps for sale
(He'd planted lots of bits of loot
To keep them on the trail.)

He sold them pirate T-shirts
A scarf, a black eye patch
Skull-and-crossbone daggers
And cutlasses to match.

They played at being pirates
They thought it was great fun
To walk the plank and dig for gold
And frolic in the sun.

They caught fish for their supper
They had to cook it too
They soon learned how to throw a shrimp
Upon the barbecue.

At night around the campfire
The coals glowed black and red
And Percy told them stories
'Til it was time for bed.

"It's been magic!" cried the tourists
"Simply magic, Percy dear
We'll tell our friends about it
And we'll come again next year!"

The island was so peaceful
Once the crowds had gone
Percy tidied up a bit
And put the kettle on.

Just Percy and his parrot
On their island, all alone
The way they really liked it
Sort of private, on their own.

And that's how we'll leave Percy
With his bald old parrot friend
I can't think of a nicer way
For Percy's tale to end.

BEFORE
Percy the Pirate
AFTER

PICTURE TALK

1. Teacher reads the poem and distributes the before-and-after pictures (page 34).
2. Children are given ample time to look at the illustrations.
3. Children discuss the differences in Percy's appearance and lifestyle.
4. Through questioning, the teacher emphasizes the changes in Percy's diet and the need to practice good health habits in the selection and preparation of food.
5. Teacher relates the subject matter to the children's personal experiences.
   Teacher asks: "Do YOU know any before-and-after people? What happened to them?"

Sarah, This Is Your Lunch

Crunch! Crunch!
Munch! Munch!
Sarah has a healthy lunch!

My Lunch

1 apple 

1 tuna and lettuce
sandwich 

1 milk 

Each of us got a good food chart showing the food groups. We had to tick what we had for lunch. I had a healthy lunch.

Sarah. Grade two.

Healthy Lunches

DESCRIPTIONS—GUESSING GAMES

1. Teacher displays Sarah's lunch box and describes one of the foods it contains. For example,

    I am a fruit.
    I am red and round.
    I am crunchy and munchy.
    I grow on a tree.
    What am I?

    - Children guess.

2. Teacher suggests "food-guide words," for example, *size, taste, texture, shape, smell, color.*

    I have two slices of fresh wholewheat bread.
    I am spread lightly with butter.
    I am filled with yummy tuna and lettuce.
    I am cut into four triangles.
    I am wrapped in plastic wrap.
    What am I?

    - Children guess.

3. Teacher helps children acquire a knowledge of food production.
    - Teacher asks: "How did the tuna fish get from the sea into Sarah's sandwich?" ("Apple from orchard," and so on.)

4. Teacher widens the subject matter to include the children's food experiences at school. For example,

    I am a milk food.
    I come in a 250 ml container.
    I have a chocolate flavor.
    What am I?

    - Children guess.
    - They consider the nutritional value of foods available at the school (if there is a canteen or food and drink machines).

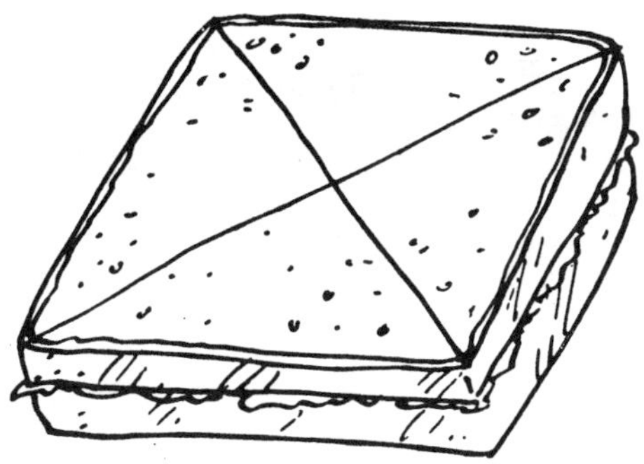

5. Children play the "lunch-guessing game" in small group or partner situations.

ROLE-PLAYING

Sarah, This Is Your Lunch

Children enjoy improvising a version of the television program *This Is Your Life.*
- Working in small groups, children role-play the contents of Sarah's lunch.
- A master of ceremonies presents each "food character" to Sarah.

Paper bag masks are useful in helping shy children gain confidence, for example,

Jonathan Apple

"Hi, Sarah. I came all the way from Farmer Brown's orchard to be in your lunch. When the men came to pick me I had to say "goodbye" to my dear old Granny Smith and then off I went in a crate to..."

(Teddy Tuna, Betty Butter, Harry Wholewheat Bread, Marvin Milk, and so on.)

Note: This activity may need teacher direction in the early stages.

RECIPE: ***Make-Your-Own-Healthy-Lunch Menu***

INGREDIENTS:

UTENSILS:

METHOD:

Shopping List

Ingredients! Ingredients!
Buy the best ingredients!
For a fun-filled food experience
The secret is...
INGREDIENTS!

Shopping

Humpty Goes Shopping

Humpty woke up. He was hungry but there was nothing to eat in the house. Humpty was not a very good housekeeper.

"Oh dear, I'll have to go shopping," he sighed. "I'm sure to forget something so I'd better make a list." Humpty couldn't write very well but he could draw, so he drew his shopping list.

• Can you guess what Humpty drew? *(Teacher draws items on blackboard. Children guess.)*

Then Humpty took his shopping list and his shopping basket and some money and toddled off down the street to Old King Cole's old corner store.

Corner Store

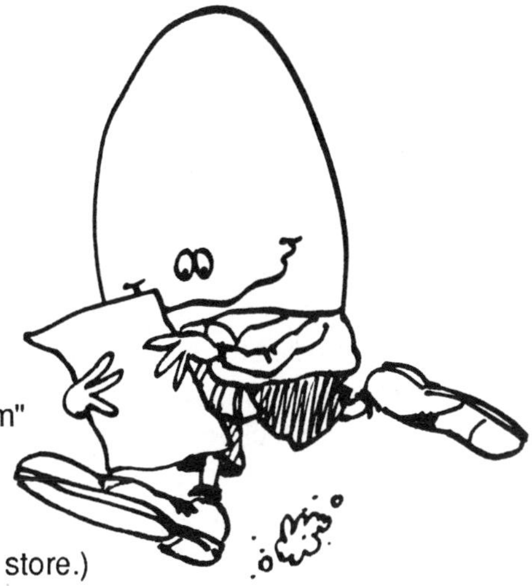

Though Humpty says
He really tries
He isn't very organized

He's not too good
At housekeeping
He's always out of everything

And so of course
He has to run
To "Old King Cole's Emporium"

(That's what it says
Above the door
Of Old King Cole's old corner store.)

A little bell goes
"Ting-a-ling"
To let him know someone's come in

It's dark inside
The floorboards creak
And naughty mice play hide-and-seek,

There are lollipop jars
And cookie tins
Maple syrup, safety pins

Candles, earrings
Kerosene
Cleaning supplies and magazines

Toffee apples
Two cents each
Ice cream cones well out of reach

Marbles, mousetraps
Pots of glue
Pens and pencils, erasers too

Sticky strips
For catching flies
Homemade lemonade to try

As Humpty says
"All this and more
At Old King Cole's old corner store!"

"Good Morning, Humpty," said Old King Cole, and he and Humpty had a cozy little chat. Then Humpty gave Old King Cole his shopping list. Old King Cole had no trouble reading Humpty's pictures, and soon the bottle of milk, the loaf of bread, and the butter and eggs and bananas were packed safely into Humpty's shopping basket.

"Will that be all, Humpty?" asked Old King Cole with a smile. (He knew Humpty had a very sweet tooth.)

"I'll just have a quick look at the candy tray, please," said Humpty.

Old King Cole brought out his candy tray. All kinds of sweets were spread out on the tray—jellybeans, mints, licorice all-sorts, striped candy canes, chocolates, and bubble gum.

"Six candies for a penny, Humpty," said Old King Cole.

Humpty chose six of his favorite sweets and Old King Cole popped them into a little white paper bag and tucked them into Humpty's shopping basket. Humpty paid for his groceries, said "goodbye" to Old King Cole and toddled off down the street to his house.

"It's lucky that a not-very-good housekeeper like me has Old King Cole's old corner store nearby," thought Humpty.

There aren't many old corner stores left now.

- Do *you* have one near your house?

SHOW AND TELL

1. Teacher reads the story. Children discuss the differences between shopping at Old King Cole's old corner store and a supermarket of today:
   –prices
   –service
   –distance from home
   –shopping hours
   –variety of goods
   –shopping patterns (weekly instead of daily)
   –packaging
2. Children draw their own supermarket shopping lists. They "show and tell" in small groups or partner situations.

LISTENING GAME—MESSAGES

- Four children go outside.
- Teacher calls in first child, and says:
  > "Please go to the store and buy one loaf of bread, one liter of milk, one dozen eggs, and one bag of potatoes."
- First child gives message to second, second to third, third to fourth, who gives message to class.
- Class recalls teacher's original message, then compares messages. (The message could be made more complicated adding quantities, qualities.)

FOLLOW-UP SHOPPING ACTIVITIES

1. Children create their own shopping center and invent its inhabitants. For example, *Mother Goose Market.*
2. Draw a wall frieze of shops. Decide who goes where, for example,

   Miss Muffet's Curds and Whey Milk Bar
   Mary, Mary's Growers' Mart
   Pat-a-Cake the Baker's Shop

3. Draw food items in the windows and create labels for imaginary contents of goods.
4. Make cards using labels such as, *jam, cocoa, peanut butter* for playing games, for example, the card game "Snap."
5. Tape TV or radio advertisements for foods and food services and mime them.
6. Adapt nursery rhymes or create originals, with food themes, for example,

CLASS: Mary, Mary
Quite contrary
How does your garden grow?

MARY: With apples and peas
And long green beans
And cauliflowers
All in a row.

7. Collect newspaper advertisements of different supermarkets. Compare prices.
8. Compile a giant class recipe book of *Nursery Rhyme Recipes.*
9. Discuss one recipe using correct terms for ingredients and utensils, precise instructions.

10. Record recipe prior to cooking session and illustrate to provide a pictorial guide.
11. Children could research and adapt recipes for the nursery rhyme theme, for example,

    Breadmaking (Pat-a-Cake the Baker)
    Scrambled Eggs (Humpty Dumpty)
    Making Yogurt (Miss Muffet)
    Jam Tarts (The Queen of Hearts)

RECIPE: **Jam Tarts**

INGREDIENTS:
2 cups flour (500 ml)
½ cup butter/margarine (125 ml)
½ teaspoon salt (2 ml)
2–3 Tbsp. cold water (30–45 ml)
strawberry or raspberry jam

UTENSILS:
mixing bowl
sieve or sifter
set of measuring spoons
fork or pastry blender
rolling pin
large round cutter
muffin tins

METHOD:
1. make short pastry—sift flour and salt into the bowl
2. cut in butter/margarine until mixture is like fine breadcrumbs
3. add cold water slowly and mix to a soft dough
4. place on floured board and knead lightly
5. roll out dough, cut out and line muffin tins
6. add a little jam to each pastry case
7. bake for 15 minutes in a hot oven (400°F or 200°C)
8. as soon as tarts are taken from oven, top up with extra jam

The Queen of Hearts' Tarts

CHARACTERS:
Queen of Hearts
King of Hearts
Knave of Hearts
Chorus

QUEEN:
Oh me! Oh my!
Look at the sky
What a lovely summer's day!

CHORUS:
What a lovely summer's day!

QUEEN:
I'll make some tarts
For the King of Hearts

KNAVE:
And I'll steal those tarts away!

CHORUS:
And he'll steal those tarts away!

QUEEN: Oh boo-hoo-hoo!
The Knave of Hearts
Has stolen all my lovely tarts!

CHORUS: He's stolen all her lovely tarts!

KING: Come here to me
You naughty Knave
That's not a nice way to behave!

CHORUS: That's not a nice way to behave!

KING: So now you must be
Beaten sore
To make quite sure you steal no more

CHORUS: To make quite sure you steal no more

KING: Take that! And that!
Now fetch the tarts
And bring them to the Queen of Hearts

CHORUS: He'll bring them to the Queen of Hearts

KNAVE: I'm very sorry, Sir
I'm sure
I vow that I will steal no more

CHORUS: He vows that he will steal no more

QUEEN: At last! At last!
My lovely tarts!
Now I'm a happy Queen of Hearts

CHORUS: Now she's a happy Queen of Hearts.

Grow-Your-Own

Planting things
Planting things
Around my kitchen door.

Tending things
Tending things
To help them grow some more.

Greening things
Greening things
Where nothing grew before.

Growing things
Growing things
That's what nature's for.

Grow Your Own Food

RECIPE: ***A-Grow-Your-Own-Alfalfa-Sprouts Sandwich***

INGREDIENTS:
alfalfa seeds
enough water to moisten seeds

UTENSILS:
glass jar
J-cloth
rubber band

METHOD:
1. place seeds in jar until quarter full
2. dampen seeds (they must be kept moist)
3. place damp J-cloth on top of jar—secure with rubber band, drain off any excess water
4. place jar where it will receive sunlight
5. schedule children to water and drain seeds daily—then observe growth and keep diaries
6. when seeds have sprouted, make alfalfa sprouts sandwiches using wholewheat bread
7. serve with fruit at playtime

RECIPE: ***Alfalfa Sprouts Salad***

INGREDIENTS:
1 cup alfalfa sprouts (250 ml)
2 celery stalks
1 cucumber
3 radishes
2 apples
2 tomatoes
herbs

UTENSILS:
peelers
knives
cup
salad bowl

METHOD:
1. peel, slice, chop vegetables
2. place in a bowl— mix with alfalfa sprouts
3. add herbs—chopped parsley and chives
4. serve with a bottled salad dressing

Henrietta's Garden

It was a hot, still afternoon. In the darkened bedroom a little girl lay in a high oak bed. Her mother and sister sat beside her, fanning her gently. The little girl's name was Henrietta and she was suffering from a dreadful illness called polio. The doctors could do nothing for her because in the year 1898 there was no cure for the disease, and many children died from it.

Her parents were so anxious that they tried everything to make Henrietta well. A friend had told them that warm, dry, beach sand packed tightly about the patient's body would restore the muscles withered by the disease. So Henrietta's father and brothers drove the family horse and wagon ten miles over the old plank road and through the woods to the beach to collect the sand. But, of course, such treatment proved useless.

Henrietta was grievously frail and ill, but she was very brave in spirit, and slowly, very slowly, she began to recover. When she grew strong enough her sisters and brothers would sit with her and read to her. She was lucky to have such a large family. There were nine children in Henrietta's family—Anna, Walter, Rosa, Flora, Albert, Clara, Henrietta, Marcus, and baby Gretchen.

Their parents, Heinrich and Louise Schmidt, had left their home in Germany to begin a new life in North America. Heinrich Schmidt was a builder by trade and he built his family a comfortable home in the country close to town. Henrietta's bedroom looked out onto tall trees growing in forest. From her bed, Henrietta loved to watch the trees and the birds through her window. To help the long days pass, her parents planned little surprises for her. One day, her father brought in his toolbox and began to measure Henrietta's window.

"What are you doing, Pa?" asked Henrietta.

"We can't take you out into the garden, liebling, so we are bringing the garden to you," he said. "I am making you a window box. You will have your very own garden, Henrietta."

When the box was finished her father carried Henrietta to the window to watch her mother prepare the pots inside the box.

"Would you like to grow flowers or vegetables, Henrietta?" asked her mother. "Tomato plants would do well."

"I'd like a different kind of garden, Mutti," said Henrietta. "I think I'd like an herb garden."

"What a good idea," said her mother. When you are better you'll be able to help me with the cooking and you can pick fresh herbs from your very own garden."

And that is how Henrietta's herb garden happened. As she grew stronger, Henrietta watched her herb garden grow too. And although she would never be able to run and dance as other children could, she did learn to walk again, slowly and painfully, but she always limped a little, especially when she was tired.

But she was never too tired to care for her garden. All her life she loved growing things, trees and flowers and ferns and vegetables. And always, at her kitchen window, Henrietta grew little pots of delicate, fragrant herbs.

I know she did...because Henrietta was my mother.

GROWING HERBS

Herbs are easy to grow. Most like the sun, but others prefer the shade, or indoors. Basil, chives, marjoram, parsley, and sage grow well in pots.

- Early in the new year, each child could grow an individual pot of herbs to be ready in May as gifts for Mother's Day.

MAKE A LEAFY MOTHER'S DAY CARD

1. If your leaves are already out, collect a variety of leaves, glue, paint, and markers.

2. Design the format of the leaf-card. Include a greeting, message, signature, and decoration.

3. Allow leaves to dry thoroughly before painting or printing takes place.

RECIPE: ***Eggs 'n Stuff***

INGREDIENTS:
1 medium tomato, chopped
1 teaspoon parsley, chopped (5 ml)
1 egg
2 Tbsp. butter/margarine (30 ml)
1 Tbsp. chopped onions (15 ml)
1 Tbsp. grated cheese (15 ml)
salt and pepper to taste

UTENSILS:
frying pan
set of measuring spoons
fork
bowl

METHOD:
1. Place all ingredients, except the egg, into the frying pan. Simmer gently until onion is cooked.
2. Beat egg and add to mixture. Stir until thick.
3. Eat as you would scrambled eggs or use as a sandwich filling.

Note: increase quantities as required—this recipe serves only one.

There is an old saying:
"From a tiny acorn
A mighty oak tree grows."
This story is all about an acorn...

Chicken Little

CHARACTERS: Chicken Little
Henny Penny
Cocky Locky
Ducky Lucky
Goosey Loosey
Turkey Lurky
Foxy Loxy
Chorus

SCENE: *In a wood.*

FOXY LOXY: Foxy Loxy
Is my name
And eating chickens
Is my game
I'll hide behind
A big old tree
And catch a chicken
Just for me.

CHORUS: Who should come
Along that day
But Chicken Little
On her way.

CHICKEN LITTLE: *(An acorn falls on her head. She squawks.)*
Cheep Cheep Cheep
What's happening?
I think the sky
Is falling in!
Cheep Cheep Cheep
What a terrible thing
I must run
And tell the King!

CHORUS: Who should come
Along that day
But Henny Penny
On her way.

HENNY PENNY: Cluck Cluck Cluck
What's happening?

CHICKEN LITTLE: I think the sky
Is falling in.

HENNY PENNY: Cluck Cluck Cluck
What a terrible thing!

CHICKEN LITTLE,
HENNY PENNY: We must run
And tell the King!

CHORUS: Who should come
Along that day
But Cocky Locky
On his way.

COCKY LOCKY Doodle Doo
What's happening?

CHICKEN LITTLE I think the sky
Is falling in.

COCKY LOCKY: Doodle Doo
What a terrible thing!

CHICKEN LITTLE,
HENNY PENNY,
COCKY LOCKY: We must run
And tell the King!

CHORUS: Who should come
Along that day
But Ducky Lucky
On her way.

DUCKY LUCKY: Quack Quack Quack
What's happening?

CHICKEN LITTLE: I think the sky
Is falling in.

DUCKY LUCKY: Quack Quack Quack
What a terrible thing!

CHICKEN LITTLE,
HENNY PENNY,
COCKY LOCKY,
DUCKY LUCKY: We must run
And tell the King!

CHORUS: Who should come
Along that day
But Goosey Loosey
On her way.

GOOSEY LOOSEY: Honk Honk Honk
What's happening?

CHICKEN LITTLE: I think the sky
Is falling in.

GOOSEY LOOSEY: Honk Honk Honk
What a terrible thing!

CHICKEN LITTLE,
HENNY PENNY,
COCKY LOCKY,
DUCKY LUCKY,
GOOSEY LOOSEY: We must run
And tell the King!

CHORUS: Who should come
Along that day
But Turkey Lurky
On his way.

TURKEY LURKY: Gobble Gobble Gobble
What's happening?

CHICKEN LITTLE: I think the sky
Is falling in.

TURKEY LURKY: Gobble Gobble Gobble
What a terrible thing!

CHICKEN LITTLE,
HENNY PENNY,
COCKY LOCKY,
DUCKY LUCKY,
GOOSEY LOOSEY,
TURKEY LURKY: We must run
And tell the King!

CHORUS: Who should come
Along that day
But Foxy Loxy
On his way.

FOXY LOXY: You DO look tired
You poor little things
Rest in my den
And I'll tell the King!

(All exit.)

ALL: *(Off stage, together, very loudly.)*
CHEEP CHEEP CHEEP
CLUCK CLUCK CLUCK
DOODLE DOODLE DOO
QUACK QUACK QUACK
HONK HONK HONK
GOBBLE GOBBLE GOBBLE
G-G-G-R-R-R!

FOXY LOXY: (*Enters, feathers in mouth.*)
Yum Yum Yum
What a wonderful thing!
I'm so glad
The sky fell in!

Note: Use this alternate ending if your class is easily upset.

TEACHER: And they scared FOXY LOXY so badly that he ran away!

Food Moods

How does a meal
Make you feel?

Fun With Food

RECIPE: ***Chicken Soup***

INGREDIENTS:
1 pound chicken pieces (½ kg)
4 cups water (1 L)
1 carrot
1 small onion
3 celery stalks
1 teaspoon salt (5 ml)
1 sprig parsley
pepper to taste

UTENSILS:
peelers
knives
set of measuring spoons
large cooking pot
large spoon

METHOD:
1. put chicken pieces, water and salt into pot—bring slowly to boil
2. peel vegetables, cut into small cubes
3. when liquid boils, remove froth, add vegetables and seasonings
4. simmer for 2 hours
5. remove fat
6. sprinkle with chopped parsley before serving

Little Half Chick

(rudeness and wrath lead to chicken broth)

Mother hen sat
On her nest in the sun
Out hatched her chickens
One by one
Some were brown
Some were yellow
But one little chick
Was a strange little fellow
He looked as if
He'd been cut in two
I've never seen
Such a chick, have you?
He had only one eye
And one little wing
And half a beak
The poor little thing
And only one leg
Like a thin little stick
And everyone called him
Little Half Chick
And though they all loved him
As much as could be
He never felt part
Of the family
He grew quite willful
Selfish and bold
And seldom did
As he was told
"I'm off to see
The world," said he
"This place is too dull
For someone like me."
And off he went
The very next day
His family wept
As he hopped away
He hadn't gone far
When he heard a shout
"Help me, Half Chick,
Put me out!"
There by the road
He saw a fire
It crackled and hissed

As the flames flew higher
But Half Chick said
To the fire's dismay
"Help yourself!"
And he hopped away
Later he heard
The voice of a stream
"I'm choked with weeds
Help me, please."
Half Chick merely
Shook his head
"Help yourself!"
Was all he said
A voice above
Cried "Please help me"
And there was the wind
Tangled up in a tree
Half Chick laughed
Until he cried
"Help yourself!"
He very rudely replied
He did not hear
The wild wind say
"Beware, Half Chick
I'll make you pay!"
On he hopped
For many a mile
'Til he stopped by a house
To rest a while
A woman came out
"What luck!" said she
"I'll have some
Chicken broth for tea"
She popped Half Chick
Into a pot
The water boiled
As the fire burnt hot
Half Chick hopped
From side to side
"Fire! Water!
Help!" he cried
Alas in vain
Did Half Chick plead
The fire and water
Paid no heed
And later when
The woman looked

The tasty chicken broth
Was cooked
But Half Chick, burnt
Too black to eat
Was thrown away
Into the street
"Aha!" cried the wind
And tossed him high
Up into
The bright blue sky
"I'll set you on
The highest steeple
Where you'll be seen
By all the people
And there you'll turn
And never rest
North, or south,
East or west."
And so in the sun
And snow and rain
Half Chick became
A weathervane.

DISCUSSION

Although Half Chick's mother and family loved him, he grew up selfish and willful and bold.

- Why do you think this happened?
- Mothers love their babies. See if you can match these mothers with their babies.
- Unscramble the baby animals on the left and match them with their mothers on the right.

BCU	HORSE
PGELIT	LIONESS
HKICC	DEER
UPP	DUCK
ALMB	COW
GNCYET	HEN
ANFW	SEAL
UGNDCKLI	SWAN
CFLA	CAT
OLFA	SHEEP
ETIKTN	SOW

RECIPE: **_Kisses_**

INGREDIENTS:
¾ cup butter/margarine (200 ml)
⅓ cup sugar (75 ml)
1 egg (large)
1 ½ cups of all purpose flour (375 ml)
½ teaspoon baking powder (2 ml)
2 Tbsp. milk (30 ml)
1 teaspoon vanilla extract (5 ml)
jam, any kind
icing sugar

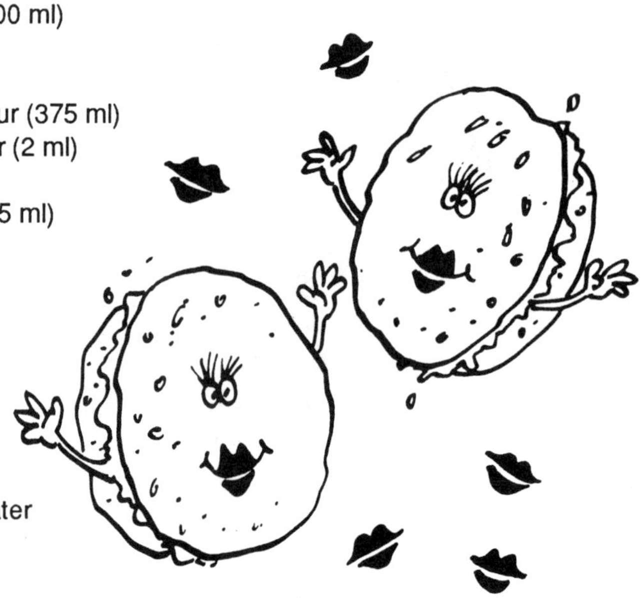

UTENSILS:
large mixing bowl
set of measuring spoons
measuring cups
sieve
greased tray
wooden spoon or hand beater
rubber spatula

METHOD:
1. cream butter and sugar
2. add egg, beat well
3. stir in vanilla extract
4. sift flour and baking powder, stir into mixture, adding milk at the same time
5. drop teaspoons of mixture onto greased tray
6. bake at 350°F (180°C) for ten minutes
7. when cool, stick two together with jam and sprinkle with icing sugar

Five Hugs a Day

(a story about love and kisses)

Once upon a time there lived a little boy. His name was Howard and he was a prince. His mother had died when he was born and his father, the king, was too busy to look after him properly.

But the king was worried about his little boy so he asked his old nanny if she would look after Howard for him. And of course she agreed.

"What a sad, lonely little boy he is," thought Nanny when she met Howard. "He doesn't know how to love. I must help him to learn."

So after that, every morning when Howard woke up, the first thing he saw was Nanny sitting by his bed in her rocking chair, knitting quietly.

And Nanny would get up, give him a kiss and a cuddle, and whisper in his ear,

"Five hugs a day
Five hugs a day
A kiss and a cuddle
And five hugs a day."

And always, every day, Nanny gave Howard more kisses and cuddles. Last thing at night, after his bedtime story and chat, Nanny would give Howard his last kiss and cuddle. Then she would settle down by his bed in her rocking chair and knit quietly while he went to sleep.

Then one morning, Howard woke up very early. Nanny was sitting by his bed as usual, but she was fast asleep. Something inside Howard's heart told him what to do. Very quietly he got out of bed and tiptoed up to Nanny's rocking chair and stood there waiting for her to wake up, and when she did...Howard gave Nanny a kiss and a cuddle and whispered in her ear,

"Five hugs a day
Five hugs a day
A kiss and a cuddle
And five hugs a day."

Howard had learned how to love, and it wasn't long before Howard was giving Nanny more than five hugs a day.

- Do **YOU** give the people you love lots of hugs and kisses?

RECIPE: ***Gingerbread Goblins***

INGREDIENTS:
- 1 cup butter/margarine (250 ml)
- ½ cup brown sugar (125 ml)
- 1 egg (beaten)
- ¼ cup molasses (50 ml)
- 2 cups all purpose flour (500 ml)
- ¼ teaspoon salt (1 ml)
- 1 teaspoon baking soda (5 ml)
- 1 teaspoon cinnamon (5 ml)
- 1 Tbsp. ground ginger (15 ml)
- 1 teaspoon cinnamon (5 ml)
- raisins
- currants

UTENSILS:
- large saucepan
- set of measuring spoons
- measuring cups
- sieve
- wooden spoon
- bowl
- rubber spatula
- rolling pin
- cookie cutters
- cookie sheet

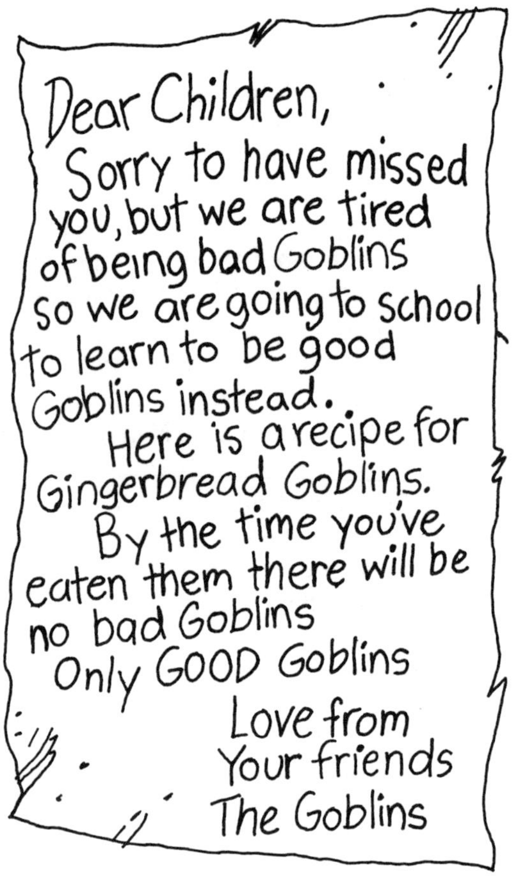

METHOD:
1. melt butter and molasses in saucepan; let cool
2. add sugar and beaten egg
3. sift together flour, baking soda, salt, cinnamon, and ginger; add to wet ingredients
4. mix well and roll onto a floured board
5. use biscuit cutters to cut face-shapes
6. use raisins and currants to create goblin faces
7. place on greased cookie sheet
8. bake at 375°F (190°C) for 10–12 minutes
9. allow to cool before removing from tray

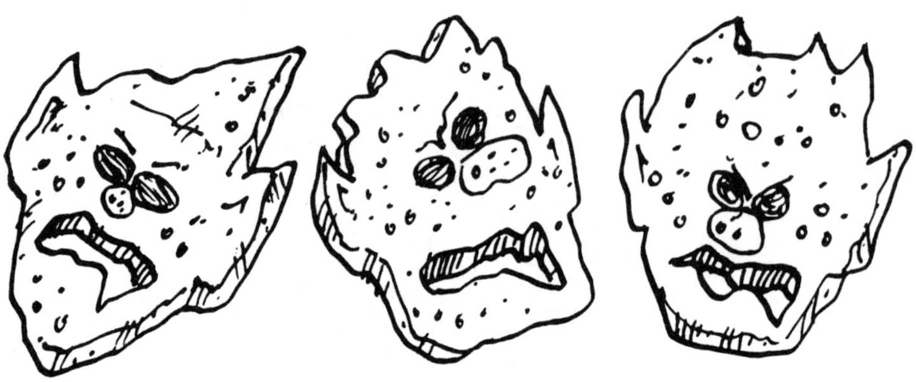

That's Disgusting!

Tony's always telling tales
That's disgusting!

Aaron doesn't share his toys
That's disgusting!

Dominic makes a dreadful noise
That's disgusting!

Esmerelda bolts her food
That's disgusting!

David's very often rude
That's disgusting!

If they learnt to mend their ways
Then we wouldn't have to say...
That's disgusting!

GROUP DISCUSSION—"BAD HABITS"

1. Teacher reads the poem, comments: "When my Grandmother bolted her food like Esmerelda, she was made to chew each mouthful TWENTY times!"
2. Teacher asks: "What other bad habits do children have?"
   - At school (not taking turns, not "going out" when playing games, teasing other children).
   - At home (borrowing things without asking, not doing one's share of household jobs, arguing about TV programs.)
3. Children move into groups of four. They discuss the worst "bad habit" they know, and what can be done to correct it.
4. Each group selects its best idea and reports to the class.

RECIPE: **_Melting Moments_**

INGREDIENTS:
1 cup butter/margarine (250 ml)
⅓ cup icing sugar (75 ml)
2 cups flour (500 ml)
¼ cup cornstarch (50 ml)

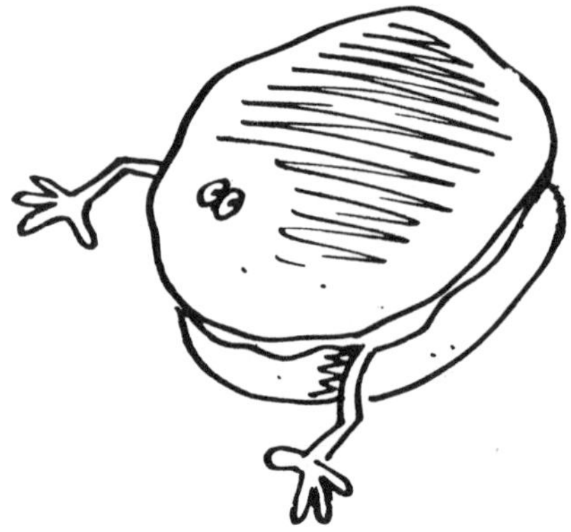

UTENSILS:
1 large mixing bowl
sieve
set of measuring spoons
measuring cups
wooden spoon or hand beater
rubber spatula
greased tray
fork

METHOD:
1. cream butter, beat in icing sugar until fluffy
2. sift flour and cornstarch together—combine with butter mixture
3. roll into balls, place on greased tray, press down with fork
4. bake in moderate oven—350°F (180°C) until golden brown (about 15 to 20 minutes)
5. when cold, stick two together with filling

FILLING:
4 Tbsp. icing sugar (50 ml)
1 Tbsp. butter/margarine (melted) (15 ml)
1 Tbsp. milk (15 ml)
1 Tbsp. vanilla extract (15 ml)

Mix all ingredients to make a creamy mixture.

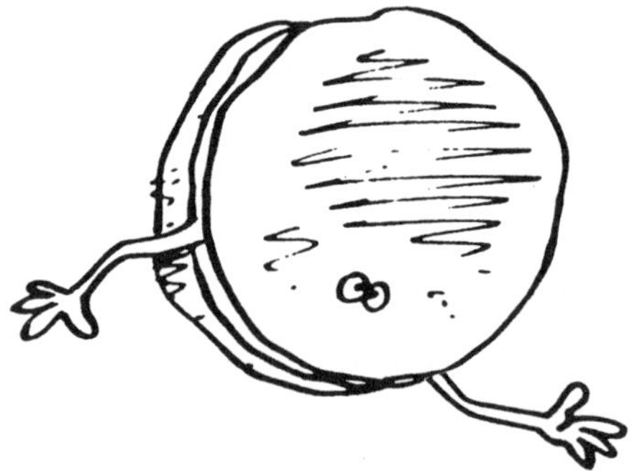

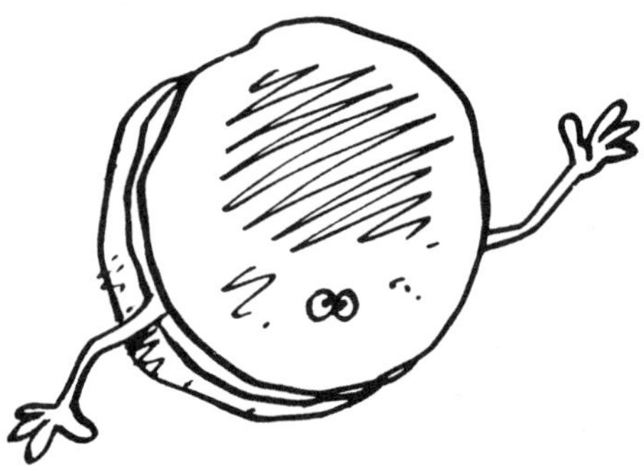

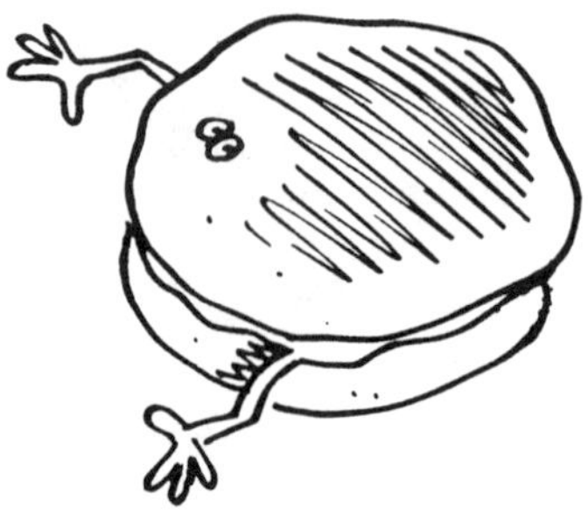

Beauty and the Beast

(a story for "Melting Moments")

There once lived a very rich merchant. He was so rich he was able to give his daughters everything they wished for and more. But one day misfortune befell him. Sad at heart, he called his anxious children to him.

"My beloved children," he said. "My treasure ships have all been lost at sea. I shall have to sell our fine home to pay my debts. All I have left is an old cottage in the country. We will have to live there."

His daughters, except for Beauty who was the youngest, cried out in dismay, "Live in the country! Leave our friends! And not have any servants to look after us!"

"I am afraid so, my dears," said their father sorrowfully.

Only Beauty felt sympathy for her unhappy father and she kissed him lovingly.

"We must make the best of it," she said hopefully.

A year passed. The merchant and his family lived an unhappy, lonely life in the tumbledown cottage. The merchant's daughters, except for Beauty, complained bitterly all day long.

Then one morning the merchant received news that one of his treasure ships had arrived safely in port.

The girls were delighted! How they longed to be rich again. They begged their father to bring them back jewels and gowns and trinkets. Beauty asked for nothing.

"Just bring yourself home safely, Father," she said as she kissed him fondly.

"Don't worry about me, my dear," said her father, "but do choose something for yourself, my dear girl."

"Well, Father," said Beauty rather sadly, "just bring me back a rose, like the ones we used to grow at home."

"A rose it shall be!" cried her father, and in happy spirits he set off eagerly on his journey.

But to his despair, he found that the wicked captain of his ship had stolen all the treasure and disappeared.

Sad at heart, the merchant turned towards home, poorer than ever.

A wild storm arose and he was forced to seek shelter in a deserted castle.

"What splendor! What richness!" thought the merchant as he wandered through the great empty chambers. At last he fell asleep before a roaring fire. When he awoke a delicious breakfast was waiting for him on the table.

Through the window he saw roses growing in the garden. He plucked one for Beauty. Then he froze in terror.

A fearful sound was heard...muffled roars and mutterings, and heavy dragging footsteps, and there appeared before the terrified merchant the most terrible, hideous Beast.

The merchant fell on his knees and babbled his story to the Beast.

"I shall spare your life, you thief," roared the Beast, "on one condition. You must give me one of your daughters, and she must come to me of her own free will. If she does not, you must return to me yourself."

The merchant was too terrified to argue.

When he reached home he told his distressed children what had befallen him.

"Now I must bid you all farewell and return to the Beast," he said, gathering his daughters tenderly in his arms.

"I shall go in your place, Father," said Beauty. "It was I who asked for the rose."

"That cannot be, my dearest child," said the merchant.

"Dearest Father, I insist," said Beauty bravely.

"Then we shall go together," said her father.

The Beast was waiting.

"Did you come willingly?" he asked Beauty quietly.

"Yes, Sir," she whispered.

"Then you are a brave girl," said the Beast. "Merchant, you may return home. In the stables you will find horses laden with gold. You will never be poor again. Now, leave us."

Beauty clung to her father lovingly, then, his eyes blinded with tears, the merchant departed.

"Do you find me ugly, Beauty?" asked the Beast wistfully.

"I do not wish to hurt your feelings, Sir, but I cannot tell a lie," said Beauty fearfully.

"Could you ever marry me, Beauty? Come, do not be afraid to tell me," said the Beast kindly.

"No, sir," whispered Beauty.

"You are a brave girl," said the Beast sadly. "We will not speak of it again." And he kept to his word.

Although Beauty was quite happy living at the Beast's castle she longed to see her family. One day the Beast found her crying bitterly.

"What is wrong?" he asked. "What more can I do to make you happy?"

"Dear Beast, you are kind and gentle and thoughtful to me, but I beg you, let me go home, just for one week. When I return, I will stay with you forever."

The Beast was heartbroken but he let Beauty go. He gave her a gold ring, and put it gently on her finger.

"Turn this ring when you wish to return," he told her.

Her family greeted her with delight, but—strangely—Beauty found that she was missing the Beast dreadfully and that night she woke in fright. She had dreamed that the Beast was dying.

She roused her family, fondly bade them farewell, turned the ring on her finger and instantly was back in the castle.

She searched frantically for the Beast. There he lay, very still and faint, in the garden.

Beauty took him in her arms. "Oh, he is dead," she cried in despair. "I should never have left him. Dearest Beast, I love you so."

The Beast slowly opened his eyes.

"Can you love someone as ugly as I am?" he asked her faintly.

"I love you with all my heart," cried Beauty.

"Then...will you marry your loving Beast?" he asked.

"Of course I will, dearest Beast," said Beauty. And as she spoke, the Beast disappeared and in his place stood a handsome, smiling Prince.

"But where is my dear Beast," cried Beauty sadly.

"I was your Beast," said the Prince. "Because you loved me for myself alone even though I was fierce and ugly, your love broke the wicked spell that turned me into a beast."

The Prince looked lovingly at Beauty. He took her hands in his.

"Will you marry your Prince, Beauty?" he asked tenderly.

"If you are as kind and loving as my dear Beast," said Beauty, "I will marry you."

So the Prince sent for Beauty's father and sisters. They wept with joy when they saw how happy Beauty was.

The Beauty and the Prince were married with much rejoicing and together they lived in love and happiness forever after.

REFLECTION

1. Beauty's father and sisters wept with joy when they saw how happy Beauty was.
   - What things make you cry?
   - What do other people say or do when they see you crying?
   - Have you ever seen one of your friends cry?
   - Why were they crying?
   - How did you feel?
   - What did you do?
   - What did your friend do then?

2. Beauty was as loving and kind as she was beautiful. Even though she thought the Beast was ugly she tried not to hurt his feelings.
   - How would you have felt about the Beast?
   - Was the Beast as frightening as he seemed?

3. I know a little girl called Sarah who is very like Beauty. When a new child called Noriko came into Sarah's class, Sarah was very thoughtful and caring towards her. Noriko was Japanese and could not speak English. She felt lonely and frightened and strange.
   - How do you think Sarah helped Noriko?
   - Do you know any one like Sarah? Who?

4. Discuss the words from the story and the emotions the children feel when they hear these words: *sad, anxious, dismay, afraid, sorrowful, sympathy, unhappy, hopefully, lonely, delighted, fondly, worry, happy, eagerly, despair, terrified, fearful, tenderly, lovingly, bravely, quietly, wistfully, kindly, gently, thoughtfully, heartbroken, fright, fondly, love, happiness.*

A Holiday Wedding

The children in grade three were very excited. It would soon be the school holidays, and they were excited about that, of course, but something else was going to happen to make them excited. Their teacher, Miss Shepherd, was going to be married in the holidays.

Mrs. Young, the other grade-three teacher, helped the children in Miss Shepherd's class to write letters to Miss Shepherd, wishing her a happy wedding. The letters were made into a wedding book and the children gave it to Miss Shepherd. She loved it. This is Shane's letter.

Deer Miss shepherd I hope you have a wonderful weding and when you go up to the priest and when he says kise dont fget to shut your eyes.

Shane

- Have *you* ever been to a wedding?
- Let's talk about weddings. (Invitations, gifts, ceremony, reception, food!)

RECIPE: **_Animal Cookies_**

INGREDIENTS:

$\frac{2}{3}$ cup sugar (150 ml)
$\frac{1}{2}$ cup butter/margarine (125 ml)
1 egg
1 egg white
1 teaspoon lemon juice (5 ml)
1 teaspoon vanilla extract (5 ml)
3 $\frac{3}{4}$ cups all purpose flour (925 ml)
1 teaspoon baking soda (5 ml)
1 egg yolk
1 Tbsp. milk (15 ml)
additional flour for cutting board

UTENSILS:

1 large mixing bowl
1 medium mixing bowl
set of measuring spoons
measuring cups
wooden spoon or hand beater
rolling pin
cookie cutters (animal shapes)
pastry brush

METHOD:

1. preheat oven to 400°F (200°C)
2. mix sugar, butter, egg, egg white, vanilla extract, and lemon juice
3. combine flour and baking soda
4. knead the flour and soda gradually into the first mixture
5. roll out on floured cutting board
6. cut into animal shapes
7. brush with mixture of egg yolk and milk
8. bake in preheated 400°F (200°C) oven for 10 minutes or until golden brown

The Four Musicians of Bremen

(a story of animal friendship)

CHARACTERS:

Donkey	Three Robbers
Dog	Storytellers
Rooster	Chorus
Cat	

SCENE ONE: *On the road to Bremen.*

STORYTELLERS: *(Enter left)*
The folk in this tale
Have no fathers or mothers
Or aunts or uncles
Or sisters or brothers
Or grandpas or grandmas
Or cousins or others
And nobody loves them at all.

CHORUS: And nobody loves them at all.

DONKEY: *(Enters right, moves center)*
I am an old donkey
I'm feeble and weary
I try to be strong
And I try to be cheery
But sometimes I'm tired
And sometimes I'm teary
And nobody loves me at all.

CHORUS: And nobody loves him at all.

DOG: *(Enters right)*
Though I'm an old doggie
I once was a hound dog
A run-jump-and-leap dog
A three-meter-bound dog
But now I'm an old dog
A put-in-the-pound dog
And nobody loves me at all.

CHORUS: And nobody loves him at all.

ROOSTER: *(Enters left, moves center)*
As King of the Farmyard
My voice was so splendid
But now it's all croaky
And cannot be mended
And I am afraid
For the pot I'm intended
And nobody loves me at all.

CHORUS: And nobody loves him at all.

CAT: *(Enters left)*
When I was a cool cat
A tails-and-top-hat cat
No mouse could escape
Such a quick off-the-mat cat

It's sad that I'm now
A goodbye-to-all-that cat
And nobody loves me at all.

CHORUS: And nobody loves him at all.

DONKEY: To sum up, my friends
We've no fathers or mothers

DOG: Or aunts or uncles

ROOSTER: Or sisters or brothers

CAT: It's clear to me, friends
That we just have each other.

ALL: It's lucky we met here at all.

CHORUS: It's lucky they met here at all.

DONKEY: I'm going to Bremen
To start up a band there.

DOG: I'd like to come too
I could give you a hand there.

ROOSTER: Oh, take us, please do!
It sounds perfectly grand there.

ALL: We'll start a new life for us all.

CHORUS: They'll start a new life for them all.
(Exit left)

SCENE TWO: *At the Robber's House.*
A table, set for dinner, and four chairs are to the right. Three robbers, seated at the table, are counting coins from money bags.

STORYTELLERS: *(Enter left)*
By nightfall the four friends
Were hungry and tired
They stopped at a house
Where inside by the fire
Three robbers were counting
The loot they'd acquired
But our friends weren't frightened at all.

CHORUS: But our friends weren't frightened at all.

ANIMALS: *(Enter left, limping. See the robbers, react.)*
Let's all sing together
We'll hee-haw and bow-wow
And holler and bellow
And doodle and meow-meow

STORYTELLERS:
The three robbers fled
From the ear-splitting loud row
Perhaps they won't come back at all.

CHORUS:
Perhaps they won't come back at all.
(Robbers exit right)

STORYTELLERS:
(Animals eat supper, keep watch)
That night after supper
The friends were not sleeping
Instead through the night
Wide awake they were keeping
And when from the forest
The robbers came creeping
The friends were prepared, one and all.

CHORUS:
The friends were prepared, one and all.

STORYTELLERS:
(Robbers enter right, one at a time)
The first robber came
And the old donkey kicked him
The second one came
And the old doggie bit him
The third robber came
And the other two hit him
And that was the end of them all.

CHORUS:
And that was the end of them all.
(Robbers exit right)

DONKEY:
We've made up our minds

DOG:
Yes, we've made our decisions

ROOSTER:
We won't go to Bremen

CAT:
We won't be musicians

ALL:
We now have a home
And we now have provisions
(Wave money-bags)

ALL:
And jolly good luck to us all.

CHORUS:
And jolly good luck to them all.

Something to think about:
If something like this
Should happen to you
And nobody wanted you
What would *you* do?

Melting Pot

Here we go
In the melting pot
Stir us around
'Til we're bubbling hot
All join in
Ready or not
Around the world
In the melting pot!

Germany

RECIPE: ***Potato Salad From Germany***

INGREDIENTS:
4 red potatoes
1 Tbsp. chopped green onions or chives (15 ml)
1 cup cooked ham, diced (250 ml)
½ cup celery, chopped (125 ml)
3 teaspoons finely chopped parsley (15 ml)
salt and pepper to taste
½ cup salad dressing (125 ml)

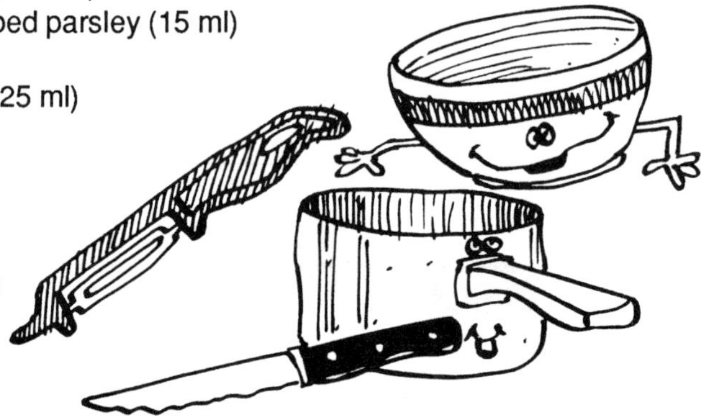

UTENSILS:
peelers
knife
large saucepan
set of measuring spoons
large spoons for mixing
bowl

METHOD:
1. peel and cook potatoes (do not overcook)—strain and leave until just cool enough to handle, but *not* cold (potato salad must be mixed when hot)
2. chop onions or chives, parsley, celery
3. cube ham
4. cube potatoes—add other ingredients and toss lightly with salad dressing
5. leave until very cold—garnish with parsley

SALAD DRESSING: Combine well
⅔ cup mayonnaise or mayonnaise-type salad dressing (150 ml)
½ teaspoon dry mustard (2 ml)
¼ teaspoon paprika (1 ml)

Rapunzel

(a folk tale from Germany)

Once, long ago
In a deep dark wood
A lonely little cottage stood.

Sleeping flowers
Drooped their heads
Vegetables dozed in their warm earth beds.

Sprigs of rapunzel
Sweetly grew
A poor man stole a leaf or two.

The flowers woke!
A witch appeared!
The poor man trembled in his fear.

"My wife is sick
We have nothing to eat
The rapunzel looked so fresh and sweet."

"I'll spare your life,"
The old witch smiled
"Just promise me your firstborn child."

Fearfully,
The man agreed,
The old witch clapped her hands in glee.

And sure enough
Without delay
When the babe was born, she took it away.

"I'll call you *Rapunzel*"
The old witch said
As she tucked the baby into bed.

The child grew winsome
Loving and sweet
With long gold hair down to her feet.

But the day would come
When the child was grown
She'd wish to have a life of her own.

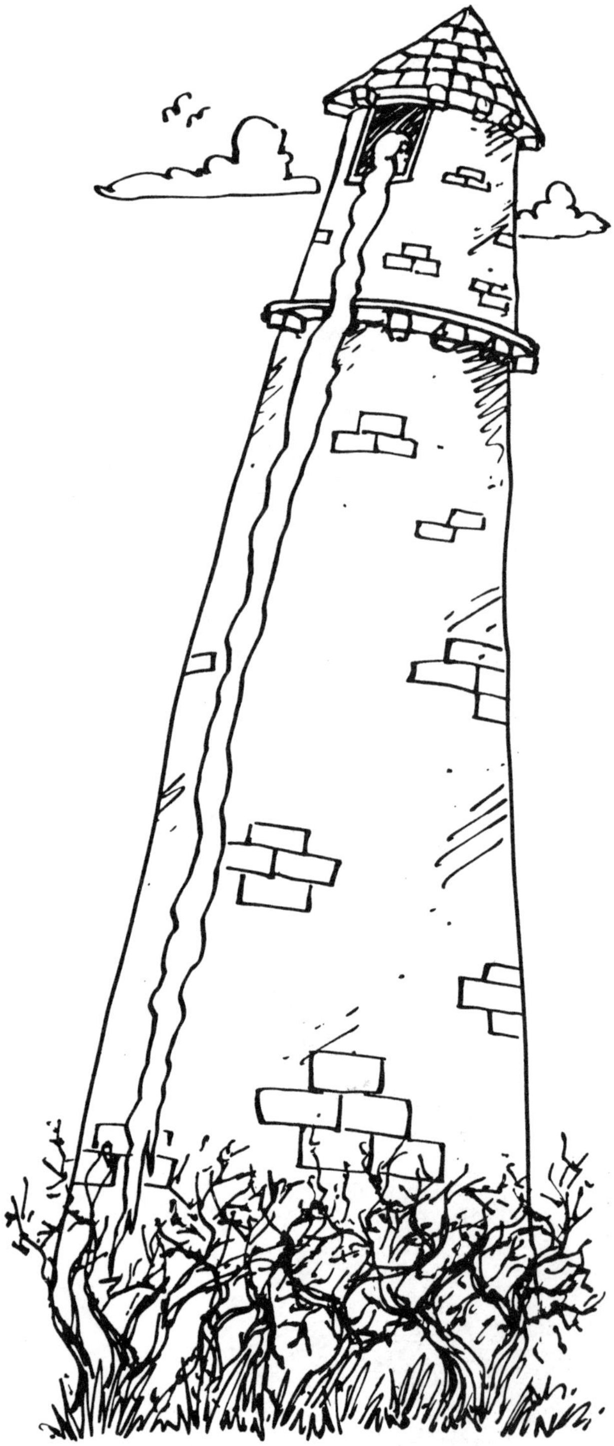

The old witch knew
And was afraid
And so a wicked plan she made.

She took Rapunzel
All through the wood
To where a great high tower stood.

And there she locked
The child away
And there poor Rapunzel had to stay.

The tower had
No stair or door
Only a window, high in the wall.

And the witch would call
From the high wall there
"Rapunzel, Rapunzel, let down your hair."

And down Rapunzel's hair
Would softly fall
And up the wicked witch would crawl.

Rapunzel's life
Was hard to bear
But nobody knew, so nobody cared.

Until one day
A prince rode by
When what should he see, but a witch appear!

He heard her call
To someone there
"Rapunzel, Rapunzel, let down your hair."

The prince returned
The very next day
To seek the songbird, hidden away.

He called aloud
To the window there
"Rapunzel, Rapunzel, let down your hair!"

Up he climbed
To the tower above
He found Rapunzel, and fell in love.

But after him
With cunning stealth
Climbed…the wicked witch herself!

She cast the prince
Far, far away
In a thorn-tree wood, near death he lay.

Rapunzel was banished
In disgrace
To a lonely, desolate place.

When the prince awoke
He could not see
Blinded by the cruel thorn trees.

He cried for Rapunzel
"Rapunzel!" he cried
Stumbling, searching, far and wide.

For days and days
He wandered on
Until he heard a faint sweet song.

He'd chanced upon
The very place
Where Rapunzel languished, in disgrace.

She flew to his arms
With loving cries
Her tears of joy healed his eyes.

He took her home
To be his wife
And kept her safe, for the rest of her life.

So ends the story
We have shared…
Rapunzel and her long gold hair.

READING FOR INFORMATION

How this folk tale got its name...

Rapunzel is a vegetable like a turnip that comes from Germany. Its bright green leaves are used in salads.

READING FOR ENJOYMENT

Other German folk tales to be told or read include:

The Wolf and the Seven Little Kids
The Elves and the Shoemaker
The Four Musicians of Bremen
The Frog Prince
Hansel and Gretel
Snow White and Rose Red
Snow White and the Seven Dwarfs
The Fisherman and his Wife
Rumpelstiltskin
One Eye, Two Eyes, and Three Eyes
The Goose Girl

China

RECIPE: ***Chinese Fried Rice***

INGREDIENTS:
1 cup long grain rice (250 ml)
2 cups water (500 ml)
4 Tbsp. oil (canola is best) (60 ml)
2 Tbsp. chopped onion (30 ml)
2 eggs, beaten
1/2 cup sliced mushrooms (125 ml)
1/2 cup green pepper (125 ml)
1/2 cup frozen peas (125 ml)
1/2 cup cooked ham or chicken, diced (125 ml)
salt

UTENSILS:
large frying pan
set of measuring spoons
knives/fork
bowl
whisk

METHOD:
1. boil water, add rice, stirring slowly until water returns to a boil
2. reduce heat, cover, and cook until rice is tender (about 15 minutes)
3. heat oil in frying pan, add chopped onion, eggs, and green pepper
4. stir with fork until egg forms small pieces
5. add remaining ingredients and mix
6. add cooked rice and continue heating and stirring until all is hot
7. season with soy sauce

Two of Everything

(a folk tale from China)

Old Mr. and Mrs. Hak-Tak were very poor. They lived in a tiny cottage in a tiny village on the side of a mountain in China.

One day, old Mr. Hak-Tak was working in his tiny vegetable patch when he bumped his big toe on something hard. Old Mr. Hak-Tak who was rather testy and touchy at the best of times, became very agitated. He gave the hard thing a kick with his other foot and hurt his other big toe as well. As he jumped about in pain and rage, he dislodged the hard something and, looking down, he saw it was a fine brass pot. At the end of the day he took it home to his wife who was cooking rice for their supper.

"What have you there, Husband?" she cried. Her eyesight was poor, so she stood very close to the pot and peered into it. Her hair-comb, the only one she owned, fell into the pot. Old Mrs. Hak-Tak put her hand inside the pot to retrieve her hair-comb, and to her great amazement, she brought forth not one, but *two* hair-combs!

"Husband, Husband," she cried, "this is a very strange pot indeed."

Old Mr. Hak-Tak bent over the pot to examine it more closely. As he did so his old leather wallet which contained the few coins they possessed, fell from his pocket into the pot.

"Fetch it out, fetch it out," cried old Mrs. Hak-Tak, who was usually a gentle, timid soul but who was now sparkling with excitement.

"Look, Wife!" cried the old man, "my old wallet, and a new wallet, with the same number of coins in each! We are rich!"

"Let us put in this sack of rice," cried old Mrs. Hak-Tak, "and see what happens!"

Soon they had two sacks of rice!

"Put in the kettle—and the teapot—and the bed quilt—and my best hat!" (her only hat) cried Mrs. Hak-Tak.

"And the hairbrush—and the hammer—and my warm coat!" (his only coat) cried old Mr. Hak-Tak.

The pot gave forth two of everything.

Old Mr. and Mrs. Hak-Tak sat down to rest.

"Husband," said old Mrs. Hak-Tak, "we do not need two teapots and two hammers and two kettles."

"That is so," agreed old Mr. Hak-Tak.

"But," suggested old Mrs. Hak-Tak, "we do need..."

"Money," said her husband.

"Yes," said his wife, "if we take the coins from the two wallets and throw them into the pot, we will have doubled our money!"

They had a lovely time playing this game and soon a large pile of coins lay on the kitchen floor. They forgot all about the rice that was cooking for their supper.

The next morning old Mr. Hak-Tak took some of the money and went into the village to buy some goodies. Old Mrs. Hak-Tak cleaned the tiny cottage and put some rice on to cook.

"I hope our pot is still working," she said, and she dropped a cabbage leaf into the pot. Sure enough, she pulled two cabbage leaves from the pot.

She fetched a cloth, and bent down to dust the pot. At that moment old Mr. Hak-Tak arrived, laden with goodies. He startled old Mrs. Hak-Tak and she fell head-over-heels into the pot! With much huffing and puffing he pulled her out. She gave a scream...and pointed. Two thin little legs, just like her own were waving about in the pot! The two old people pulled and tugged at the legs and out came a new Mrs. Hak-Tak, exactly the same as the old Mrs. Hak-Tak!

"What shall we do with her?" asked old Mr. Hak-Tak, "I already have one wife."

The new Mrs. Hak-Tak stood there looking very unwanted and unhappy.

"Put her back in the pot!" she cried in a not-very-gentle, not-very-timid manner.

"You silly woman!" shouted old Mr. Hak-Tak in his most testy, touchy manner, "then there will be three Mrs. Hak-Taks!" He jumped up and down in his agitation, lost his balance, and fell into the pot himself!

The two Mrs. Hak-Taks pulled and tugged again and out came a new Mr. Hak-Tak, exactly the same as the old Mr. Hak-Tak.

"What shall I do with him?" asked old Mrs. Hak-Tak, "I already have one husband."

The new Mr. Hak-Tak stood there looking very unwanted and unhappy.

Old Mrs. Hak-Tak felt sorry for the new Mr. and Mrs. Hak-Tak. Then she had an idea. "Would you like to have supper with us?" she asked them. "There is plenty of rice for us all."

After supper, old Mrs. Hak-Tak had another idea. "We have two Mr. Hak-Taks and two Mrs. Hak-Taks," she said, so why don't we have two of everything?"

"Two of everything?" repeated old Mr. Hak-Tak.

"Yes," went on old Mrs. Hak-Tak. "The pot has been so good to us. It has given us so much. Why don't we use the money to build ourselves a new comfortable house and another one exactly the same next door for new Mr. and Mrs. Hak-Tak."

Everyone thought that was a splendid idea. So that's just what they did, and they lived in harmony for the rest of their lives.

TELEPHONING

1. Teacher reads the story and asks children, "Have you ever eaten Chinese food? Many children eat Chinese food at home. Others, enjoy going to a Chinese restaurant. Pretend it is a special occasion and you are going to a restaurant for supper."
   - Discuss dining at a restaurant, favorite foods, how to make telephone reservations.
2. Teacher revises the children's telephone techniques.
3. Children role-play a customer and restaurant owner.
4. A fluent pair of children repeat their conversation before the class, using a toy telephone.

Great Britain

RECIPE: ***Welsh Rarebit***

INGREDIENTS:
1 ½ cups cheddar cheese (375 ml)
1 Tbsp. butter/margarine (15 ml)
½ teaspoon mustard (2 ml)
2 teaspoons flour (10 ml)
2 Tbsp. milk (30 ml)
4 slices buttered toast

UTENSILS:
grater
set of measuring spoons
measuring cups
saucepan
plate
wooden spoon

METHOD:
1. grate cheese—combine in saucepan with butter/margarine, mustard, and milk
2. stir over low heat until cheese is melted and mixture is smooth
3. add flour, a little at a time, and stir until mixture thickens
4. spoon onto buttered toast—broil until golden brown and serve at once

Raggylug

(a story from Britain)

There was once a Mother Bunny
And she had a Baby Bunny
And they lived inside a burrow
Snug and cozy underground.
Every day when it was sunny
Mother Bunny left her bunny
And went to look for clover
In the fields of Farmer Brown.

"Now listen, Baby Bunny,"
Mother Bunny warned her bunny
"You must stay inside the burrow
And you must *lie low!*"
And each day the Baby Bunny
Always promised Mother Bunny
That he wouldn't move a whisker
He would just *lie low!*

But one day the Baby Bunny
Heard a noise that sounded funny
He forgot, and popped his head out
Then he cried aloud in fear.
"Mommy! Mommy! Mommy!"
Cried the frightened Baby Bunny
For a fox was there a-waiting
And it grabbed him by the ear.

From far off his Mother Bunny
Heard her frightened Baby Bunny
And she cried out, "Mother's coming!"
As across the fields she sped.
"Run quickly, Baby Bunny!"
Loudly shouted Mother Bunny
As the fox dropped Baby Bunny
And snapped at her instead.

Away ran Baby Bunny
While his clever Mother Bunny
Hopped and jumped all over
'Til the fox gave up the chase.
And then the Mother Bunny
Kissed and cuddled Baby Bunny
And they found another burrow
In a nice, safe place.

But his ear felt floppy-funny
"It won't stand up," wept the bunny
(With one ear up and one ear down
He did look rather queer.)
And all the other bunnies
Teased and laughed at Baby Bunny
They called him "Raggylug"
("Lug" is bunny-talk for ear.)

"We don't play with raggy bunnies!"
Cried all those nasty bunnies
So he played among the shadows
While they frolicked in the sun.
It was there the lonely bunny's
Floppy ear heard something funny
A far-off bunny signal
"Hunter coming! With a gun!"

Now every baby bunny
Is taught by every Mommy
The DANGER bunny signal...
"Thump your back leg on the ground!"
THUMP-THUMP-THUMP went Baby Bunny
And away ran every bunny
And when the hunter got there
Not a bunny could be found.

"Hurray for Baby Bunny!"
Shouted all the happy bunnies
And his Mother Bunny hugged him
As three hearty cheers they gave.
And that's why Baby Bunny
With his ear so floppy-funny
Is known by bunnies everywhere
As "Raggylug the Brave."

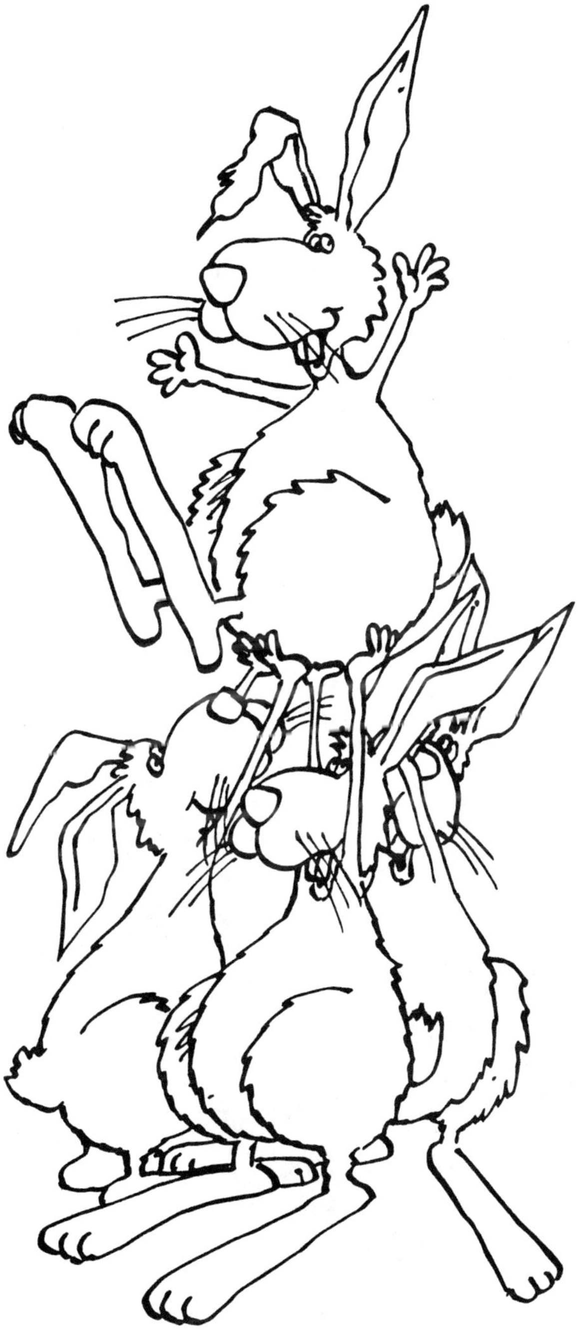

NAME GAMES

Bunny Clues

Once there was a bunny
Who had a kind of funny
Strange, peculiar, rare and different
Special sort of name.
And all the other bunnies
Thought it was quite funny
To try to guess the bunny's name
Why don't we do the same?

- This name belongs to a bunny who had a torn ear.
(Raggylug)
- This name belongs to a bunny who nearly got caught in a vegetable garden.
(Peter Rabbit)
- This name belongs to a bunny who is very busy around Easter time.
(Easter Bunny)
- This name belongs to a bunny who is always playing games on Brer Fox.
(Brer Rabbit)

Australia

RECIPE: ***Carrot Cake***

INGREDIENTS:

2 cups flour (500 ml)
½ cup brown sugar (125 ml)
½ teaspoon salt (2 ml)
1 teaspoon baking soda (5 ml)
2 teaspoons baking powder (10 ml)
1 teaspoon cinnamon (5 ml)
½ cup buttermilk (125 ml)
2 eggs, beaten
2 cups carrots, grated (500 ml)
¼ cup vegetable oil (50 ml)

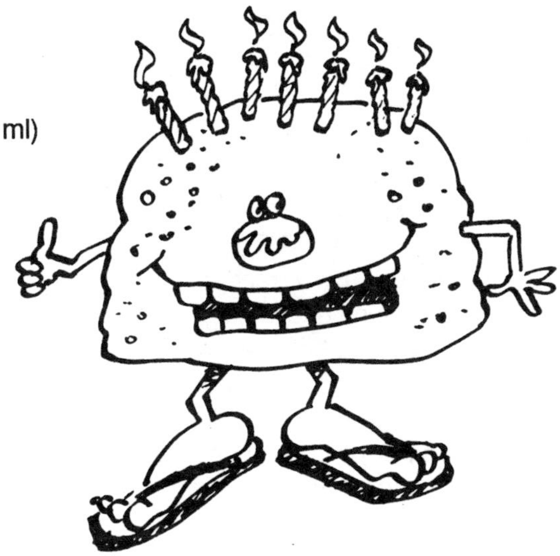

UTENSILS:

sieve
large mixing bowl
smaller bowl
measuring cup
set of measuring spoons
wooden spoon
rubber spatula
sharp knife
greased 8 ½" x 5" loaf pan (or cookie sheet)
candles

METHOD:

1. combine all the dry ingredients
2. add the grated carrots, beaten eggs, vegetable oil, and buttermilk
3. mix just until blended
4. pour into a greased loaf pan 8 ½" x 5" (or a cookie sheet, if you want to cut it in half and prepare a layer cake using ready-mix icing)
5. bake at 375°F (190°C) for 45 minutes, (325°[160°C] if using a cookie sheet), then reduce heat to moderate (350°F [180°C]) and cook a further 15 minutes
6. decorate with candles

An Australian Story

The holidays were over. Everyone was back at school. Miss Park had spent her holiday in the country and she brought "something" back with her...

The "something" was in an old shoe-box with holes poked in it so it could breathe. Miss Park told the children that the "something" was very shy and easily frightened.

They tried to guess what it was.

It was a BUNYIP! (A "bunyip" is an imaginary creature of aboriginal legend, said to live in billabongs. A "billabong" is a waterhole beside a river or creek. It is filled with water only during flood time.)

Bunyip had never been to school before. As Miss Park drove her car to school each day, Bunyip would peep out through the holes in the shoe-box. What did he see?

When Bunyip Went to School

When Bunyip went to school
Each day
What did he see (hear, read)
Along the way?
He saw a...
Along the way
When Bunyip went to school
Each day.

(Children supply, read, mime the missing word. "What did he *hear...*?" Children supply, read, make sound effects.)

Bunyip loved being at school but at night he fretted for all the other bunyips so Miss Park arranged for a friend to take him home to the bush.

On the day he left, Bunyip told Miss Park it was his birthday, so of course Miss Park's class gave him a party with balloons and presents and sausage rolls and...because Bunyip loved carrots—a carrot birthday cake!

The United States

RECIPE: ***Hamburgers***

INGREDIENTS:

1 1/2 pound ground beef (500 g)
1 egg
2 Tbsp. onion, chopped (30 ml)
1/2 teaspoon salt (2 ml)
1/2 teaspoon pepper (2 ml)
1 teaspoon worcestershire sauce (5 ml)
1 teaspoon garlic powder (5 ml)

UTENSILS:

1 large mixing bowl
set of measuring spoons
1 fork
1 sharp knife
spatula

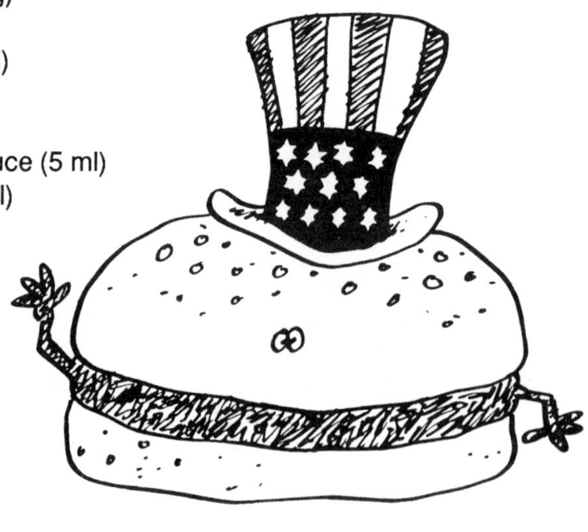

METHOD:
1. put the meat in the bowl—make a well in the center
2. add egg, onion, salt, pepper, worcestershire sauce, and garlic
3. mix together with a fork
4. place on floured surface
5. form into round shapes, 1/2 inch (1 cm) thick
6. grill for 5–8 minutes each side if burgers are thin, 10–12 minutes if they are thick (or until well done)

The Tar-Baby

(an Uncle Remus story from the southern United States)

READERS: Storyteller
Brer Fox
Brer Rabbit

STORYTELLER: Poor old Brer Fox was always trying to catch Brer Rabbit, but Brer Rabbit was too clever for him until one day...

BRER FOX: Now *this* time I is really goin' to catch that sassy Brer Rabbit. I've got me some tar and some turpentine and I is goin' to make me a Tar-Baby...just like this.

STORYTELLER: Brer Fox made the Tar-Baby, put a hat on its head, and sat in the middle of the road. Then Brer Fox lay low in the bushes nearby. Pretty soon along came Brer Rabbit, lippetty-clippetty, clippetty-lippetty.

BRER RABBIT: Why, howdy-doody! What have we here?

STORYTELLER: But the Tar-Baby, she said nothin'. And Brer Fox, he lay low.

BRER RABBIT: Good mornin'! Fine mornin', ain't it?

STORYTELLER: But the Tar-Baby, she said nothin'. And Brer Fox, he lay low.

BRER RABBIT: Is you deaf? If you is, I can *yell* louder!

STORYTELLER: But the Tar-Baby, she said nothin'. And Brer Fox, he lay low.

BRER RABBIT: You is *stuck-up*! That's what you is! If you don't say "Howdy" to me, I is goin' to *biff* you!

STORYTELLER: But the Tar-Baby, she said nothin'. And Brer Fox, he lay low.

BRER RABBIT: Well, here comes my fist to teach you some manners!

STORYTELLER: Wham! Brer Rabbit biffed the Tar-Baby with his fist and of course his fist stuck to the tar.

STORYTELLER: But the Tar-Baby, she said nothin'. And Brer Fox, he lay low.

BRER RABBIT: If you don't let loose I is goin' to *biff* you again!

STORYTELLER: But the Tar-Baby, she said nothin'. And Brer Fox, he lay low.

BRER RABBIT: Here I come then!

STORYTELLER: Wham! Brer Rabbit biffed the Tar-Baby with his other fist and that stuck too!

BRER RABBIT: Let me loose or I is goin' to *kick* the stuffin' out of you!

STORYTELLER: But the Tar-Baby, she said nothin'. And Brer Fox, he lay low.

STORYTELLER: Wham! Brer Rabbit kicked the Tar-Baby with his back paws and they stuck too!

BRER RABBIT: You'd better let me loose or I is goin' to *butt* you with my head! See how you like that!

STORYTELLER: But the Tar-Baby, she said nothin'. And Brer Fox, he lay low.

STORYTELLER: Wham! Brer Rabbit butted the Tar-Baby with his head and that stuck too! Then up sauntered Brer Fox from the bushes.

BRER FOX: Howdy, Brer Rabbit! You look a bit *stuck up* this mornin'!

STORYTELLER: Brer Fox laughed and laughed.

BRER FOX: How'd you like to come home and have dinner with me, Brer Rabbit?

STORYTELLER: Brer Rabbit knew what *that* meant and he thought very quickly.

BRER RABBIT: Take me home with you. Have me for dinner. Do what you like with me, Brer Fox, but don't throw me in the brier-patch!

BRER FOX: What did you say, Brer Rabbit?

BRER RABBIT: Drown me or hang me, Brer Fox, but please don't throw me in the brier-patch!

BRER FOX: Well, well, Brer Rabbit, so you don't want me to throw you in the brier-patch! Well, that is just what I is goin' to do with you!

STORYTELLER: And Brer Fox pulled Brer Rabbit from the Tar-Baby and threw him as far as he could into the brier-patch.

BRER FOX: Goodbye to you, Brer Rabbit!

STORYTELLER: But, quick as a wink, Brer Rabbit bobbed up out of the brier-patch and sang out to Brer Fox in a very sassy voice.

BRER RABBIT: Born and bred in the brier-patch, Brer Fox!

STORYTELLER: And Brer Fox could hear Brer Rabbit laughing as he scampered all the way home...

BRER RABBIT: Born...and...bred...in...the...brier-patch...Brer...Fox!
Born...and...bred...in...the...brier-p-a-tch!

LISTENING

Teacher prepares a story tape of "The Tar-Baby" for an appreciative listening activity. If time permits, the script could be typed on an overhead transparency for a "look and listen" session.

France

RECIPE: ***French Toast***

INGREDIENTS:
1 egg per child
1 Tbsp. milk per child (15 ml)
1 slice of bread per child
maple syrup or honey
cinnamon
butter/margarine as needed

UTENSILS:
knives
bowl
frying pan
tablespoon
whisk
spatula

METHOD:
1. cut slice of bread into quarters
2. beat egg—add a little milk and seasoning
3. melt 1 teaspoon butter/margarine in frying pan
4. dip bread pieces in egg mixture—place in frying pan
5. when one side is golden brown, turn and brown on other side
6. sprinkle with cinnamon
7. serve with maple syrup

Cinderella—a play or puppet play

(a folk tale from France)

CHARACTERS: Cinderella, 2 Ugly Sisters, Fairy Godmother, Prince, Servant, Storyteller

STORYTELLER: There was once a beautiful young girl called Cinderella. Her mother was dead and when her father remarried, his second wife and her two daughters were very cruel to Cinderella and made her their serving maid.

CINDERELLA: *(Enters, in rags, carrying a broom.)*
Oh, I'm so tired. I'll just have a little rest.
(Leans against side of stage.)

1ST UGLY SISTER: *(Off-stage)*
Cinderella! Cinderella!
(Enters)
Where is the girl? Why? What is this?

CINDERELLA: *(Wakes in fright)*
I was only having a little rest.

1ST UGLY SISTER: A rest indeed! If I see you doing that again, I shall beat you!
(Exits)

CINDERELLA: Oh dear! Oh dear! What shall I do?

2ND UGLY SISTER: *(Enters)*
Cinderella! Bring me a mirror! I must look my best for the Prince's ball.
(Cinderella exits, returns with mirror.)

2ND UGLY SISTER: Hold it still, you stupid girl! Oh, I do look charming!

1ST UGLY SISTER: *(Enters)*
Sister, aren't you ready yet?

2ND UGLY SISTER: I'm coming now, my love.
(Sisters exit.)

CINDERELLA: *(Puts down mirror, sighs.)*
Oh, how I wish I could go to the ball.

FAIRY GODMOTHER: I am your Fairy Godmother, Cinderella. I have come to grant your wish to go to the ball. Bow down your head, my dear.
(Waves wand over Cinderella.)
With my magic wand I turn you from a poor serving-maid into a beautiful princess...
(Cinderella drops below stage, then rises, dressed as a princess.)

CINDERELLA: Is this really me? Oh, thank you, Fairy Godmother!

FAIRY GODMOTHER: Just remember, you must leave when the clock strikes twelve!

CINDERELLA: I'll remember.

FAIRY GODMOTHER: Come along then dear, your carriage is waiting.
(They exit.)

STORYTELLER: *(Enters)*
The Prince danced all night with Cinderella, and fell in love with her, but as the clock struck twelve she fled from the ball, leaving one of her tiny glass slippers on the palace stairs. The Prince picked it up...
(Exits)

PRINCE: *(Enters, carrying the slipper.)*
Where has she gone? Why did she leave so quickly? I don't even know her name.

SERVANT: *(Enters)*
Excuse me, my lord, but may I make a suggestion?

PRINCE: Of course you may, my man.

SERVANT: Perhaps, my lord, we should look for the lady whose foot fits the slipper.

PRINCE: An excellent idea! We'll begin searching at dawn.
(They exit.)

STORYTELLER: *(Enters)*
The next morning Cinderella took the Ugly Sisters their breakfast.
(Exits. Cinderella enters, with tray.)

1ST UGLY SISTER: *(Seated at table.)*
I did enjoy myself last night!

2ND UGLY SISTER: What a wonderful ball it was!

1ST UGLY SISTER: And how handsome the Prince looked.

2ND UGLY SISTER: Who could that beautiful princess have been?

1ST UGLY SISTER: And why did she leave so early?

2ND UGLY SISTER: *(A knock is heard.)*
See who it is, Cinderella.

SERVANT: *(Enters, carrying the glass slipper on a cushion.)*
Good morning, ladies. My lord, the Prince wishes every lady in the land to try on this slipper. He will marry the lady whose foot the slipper fits.

1ST UGLY SISTER: Let me try first! Oooh! It's too tight for me!

2ND UGLY SISTER: Allow me, Sister! Oh dear! It's far too small for me!

SERVANT: *(To Cinderella.)*
It is your turn now, Cinderella.

1ST UGLY SISTER: Indeed it is not!

2ND UGLY SISTER: Cinderella is only a serving-maid.

SERVANT: My master desires *every* lady in the land to try the slipper.

1ST UGLY SISTER: Oh, very well.

2ND UGLY SISTER: Hurry up, Cinderella. You have work to do!

CINDERELLA: *(Tries on slipper.)*

SERVANT: Why, the slipper fits Cinderella!

1ST UGLY SISTER: Astonishing!

2ND UGLY SISTER: Amazing!

FAIRY GODMOTHER: *(Enters, waves her wand.)*
Bow your head Cinderella, and now rise, my little princess!
Cinderella drops down, rises, dressed as a princess.)

CINDERELLA: Oh, thank you, Fairy Godmother.

SERVANT: Listen...my lord, the Prince approaches.

PRINCE: *(Enters)*

SERVANT: My lord, your Princess has been found!

PRINCE: You have done well, my man, and you shall be rewarded. But where *is* the Princess?

SERVANT: She is here, my lord.

CINDERELLA: *(Moves forward, curtsies.)*
My lord.

PRINCE: My Princess! I though I had lost you! Cinderella, will you marry me?

CINDERELLA: I will.
(They embrace.)

STORYTELLER: *(Enters)*
And, as most fairy stories end, Cinderella and the Prince were married, and lived happily ever after.
(All bow.)

Special Days

Special-day recipes
Easy to cook
Are handy to have
In your class cookbook.

Easter

RECIPE: ***Hot Cross Buns***

INGREDIENTS:

1 cup all purpose flour (250 ml)
¼ cup sugar (50 ml)
3 Tbsp. butter/shortening
⅔ cup milk, warmed (150 ml)
½ cup raisins or currants (125 ml)
2 teaspoons allspice (10 ml)
1 teaspoon cinnamon (5 ml)
1 teaspoon salt (5 ml)
4 teaspoons yeast (20 ml)

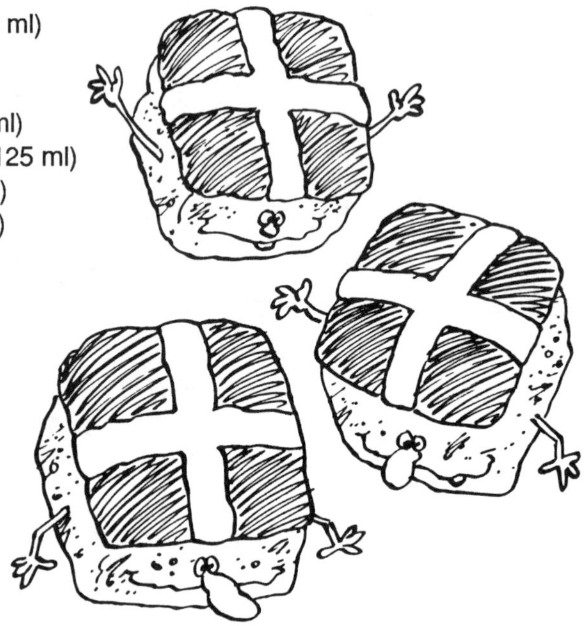

UTENSILS:

large mixing bowl
sieve
set of measuring spoons
measuring cups
fork for pastry blender
saucepan
clean paintbrush
greased tray
wooden spoon

METHOD:

1. combine flour, salt and spices in a bowl—add fruit and sugar
2. cut in butter/shortening until crumbly
3. add yeast to warm milk, leave for 10 minutes
4. pour yeast liquid into the flour mixture and stir, adding more milk if necessary
5. knead dough on floured board for 10 minutes
6. leave to rise until doubled in bulk
7. punch down, roll dough into a large sausage form
8. cut into 8 pieces, shape into rounds and press down with your hand
9. make a smooth paste from a little flour and water, brush across buns to form cross
10. cover and let stand for 15 minutes
11. bake in a hot oven (450°F [230°C]) for 15–20 minutes

RECIPE: **_Easter Egg Nests_**

INGREDIENTS:
¼ lb. cooking chocolate (100 g)
2 shredded wheat biscuits
coconut, shredded
hard-boiled or blown eggs,
or colorfully wrapped chocolate eggs

UTENSILS:
double boiler
wooden spoon
small ovenproof dish
muffin tins
paint brush
greased tray

METHOD:
1. melt cooking chocolate in ovenproof dish over a saucepan of boiling water
2. crush shredded wheat, add to melted chocolate—stir well
3. grease muffin tins—place spoonfuls of chocolate mixture into muffin tins and press the center down to form nest shapes
4. allow to set
5. paint and decorate hard-boiled or blown eggs, if used
6. remove nests from muffin tins—place eggs in nests
7. sprinkle coconut around eggs

An Easter Bunny Story

1. R-r-r-r-ring! went the alarm clock. Easter Bunny woke up. Only one week left before Easter and so much to do!
   Easter Bunny:
   –jumped out of bed
   –soaked under the shower
   –squeezed some fresh orange juice into a glass—delicious!
   –nibbled a couple of crunchy carrot tops
   –brushed his teeth
   –tidied his burrow
   AND
   –hopped down the road to his Easter egg factory
   Phew!

   • Can you remember the seven things Easter Bunny did after he woke up? Show me the first thing he did...second...third...

2. As Easter Bunny walked into his factory the clock on the wall struck eight o'clock.
   • You are factory clocks. Decide what sounds you will make and strike eight o'clock...Now!

3. Easter Bunny started the chocolate-making machines. The first machine picked up the ingredients and put them in the big mixing bowl. Easter Bunny pressed the starter button:
   p—b—t—k
   p—b—t—k
   p—b—t—k went the machine.
   • You are picking-up machines...Press your belly buttons to start... Now!

4. The second machine mixed the ingredients together. Easter Bunny flicked the switch:
   SH—z
   SH—z
   SH—z went the machine.
   • You are mixing machines...
   Press your belly buttons to start...Now!

5. The third machine was the egg-making machine. Easter Bunny pulled the lever but the machine wouldn't go! Easter Bunny was worried. "Some of the parts aren't working properly," he said. "I'll have to fix them." He set to work and soon fixed the machine.
   - You are a fixed egg-making machine...Do your parts work?
     - nod your head
       (glib-glob, glib-glob)
     - move your shoulders up and down
       (click-clack, click-clack)
     - push your arms forward and back
       (woosh-push, woosh-push)
     - stamp your feet
       (zomp-stomp, zomp-stomp)
   - Move into groups of four...Make your own egg-making machine...One part per person...Start slowly and softly...Get faster and louder...Then slower and softer...and...Stop.

6. When the chocolate was mixed, it poured down into the egg-making machine and came out as smooth, glistening, yummy, chocolate Easter eggs, ready to be wrapped in bright shiny paper. And of course Easter Bunny managed to get all the Easter Eggs ready in time for Easter!
   Good old Easter Bunny!
   Listen! There's someone at the door...who can it be?
   A basket of Easter eggs is found outside the classroom door, with a note which reads:

EXPLANATIONS

- You might like to design your own Easter-egg machine.
- Include a diagram and label each part.
- Show your invention to a partner and explain how it works.
- Invite another class to view the Easter-egg machines

World Health Day

Sick in Bed

I'm sick in bed
I'm sick in bed
I'm sick of being
Sick in bed.
My tummy hurts
And so does my head
And I'm sick of being
Sick in bed.

I'm sick in bed
I'm sick in bed
I'm sick of being
Sick in bed.
My big toe hurts
And so does my head
And I'm sick of being
Sick in bed.

I'm sick in bed
I'm sick in bed
I'm sick of being
Sick in bed.
My throat hurts
And so does my head
And I'm sick of being
Sick in bed.

I'm sick in bed
I'm sick in bed
I'm sick of being
Sick in bed.
Tummy, big toe,
Throat, ears, head
I'm sick of being
Sick in bed.

Mick Gets Sick

Mick wasn't sick very often. When he was really sick his mom or dad would pick up Mick's grandfather and bring him to their house, and Grandfather would look after Mick while his parents were at work. When Mick was only a little bit sick his parents would take him to Grandfather's house and pick him up on their way home.

"Be a good boy, Michael," they always said. They never called him "Mick," but Grandfather always did.

"Into bed, Mick, quick-sticks," Grandfather would say, as he tucked Mick into bed in his dad's old bedroom.

On the table by the bed stood Mick's dad's old tin alarm clock. Grandfather always let Mick wind the clock and tick, tick, tick it went, as good as new. In the bookcase were his dad's old storybooks and of course Grandfather let Mick pick which stories he wanted Grandfather to read to him. And on the dressing table were Mick's dad's football trophies.

"Your Dad was a good player, Mick," Grandfather would say proudly. Mick loved to hear about the things his dad had done when he was a boy.

As soon as Mick was tucked in, Grandfather would make them some cocoa in his thick old china mugs. Then after a story or two, he would fetch the pack of cards from the sideboard in the dining room and he and Mick would play "fish" and "snap." Mick would practice the card tricks his Grandfather had taught him.

Mick loved to watch his grandfather's old strong hands as he shuffled and dealt the cards. Grandfather had been a bricklayer before he had retired. He still did a few bricklaying jobs for people who wanted a fancy brick fireplace or a barbecue or a garden wall built. But most of the time Grandfather just picked the odd caterpillar off his vegetables and went fishing.

Grandfather had lots of visitors. Old Dick Smith who lived down the road usually stopped for a chat on his way to the shop. He always had a new "knock-knock" joke to tell Mick. And Mrs. Hicks, Grandfather's next door neighbor often popped in with a plate of hot muffins for breakfast.

On the days when Mick was only a little bit sick, almost better in fact, he helped Grandfather cook their lunch.

"Shepherd's pie and bread pudding for dinner today, Mick,' said Grandfather. "There's some chicken soup, too." Grandfather always had a hot midday dinner. (Grandfather called lunch "dinner," and dinner "supper.")

"And later this afternoon we'll go down to the garden and pick some strawberries. Then we'll make some strawberry jam," Grandfather went on.

"Great," said Mick. He'd never made strawberry jam before.

No wonder Mick loved going to Grandfather's house. "It was worth getting sick," thought Mick.

THE "I HEAR" GAME

Teacher reads the story.

- Teacher and children play the "I hear" game.

For example: I hear
With my little ear
Something ending
With..."ick."

1. This is a story about a boy called...
2. Grandfather often looked after Mick when Mick was...
3. At Grandfather's house Mick wound up his dad's old tin clock, and it went...
4. Grandfather taught Mick a new card...
5. Grandfather made cocoa in china mugs that were old and...
6. One of Grandfather's friends was called...Smith.

- Do we have anyone with an "ick" name in our class? What sort of food do *you* eat when you are sick?
- Do *you* know any old-fashioned recipes like Mick's grandfather's? See if you can find some. You could start with strawberry jam.

RECIPE: ***Grandfather's Shepherd's Pie***

INGREDIENTS:
1 large onion, minced
1 pound ground beef or lamb (500 g)
salt and pepper to taste
1 teaspoon parsley, chopped (5 ml)
1 can crushed tomatoes
2 Tbsp. flour (30 ml)
2 cups frozen green beans, steamed (500 ml)
2 carrots, diced
2 celery stalks, chopped
4 potatoes, cooked
½ cup milk (125 ml)
1 Tbsp. margarine/butter (15 ml)
1 egg beaten

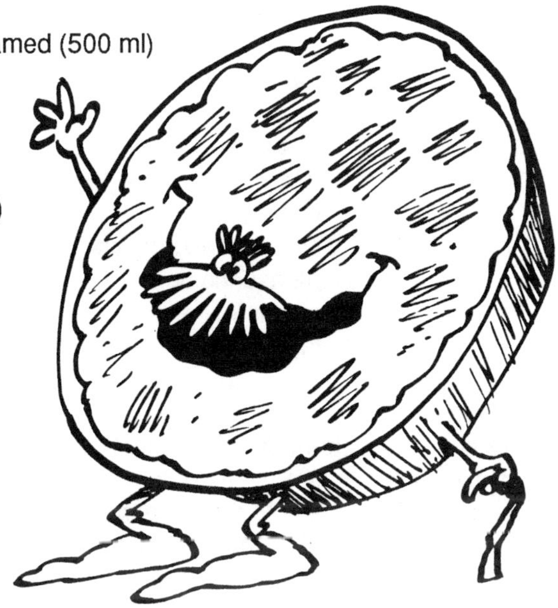

UTENSILS:
large frying pan
set of measuring spoons
peeler
wooden spoons
knife
potato masher
large casserole dish

METHOD:
1. chop onion finely
2. cook meat and onion in saucepan until brown
3. add salt and pepper
4. stir in beans, carrots, celery, and tomatoes
5. add parsley, sprinkle flour over mixture then stir
6. pour mixture into greased casserole dish
7. peel, cook, and mash potatoes
8. add milk, margarine/butter, beaten eggs, and pepper
9. arrange potatoes over meat mixture
10. bake in 350°F (180°C) oven for 45 minutes until the top is crisp and lightly browned

RECIPE: ***Grandfather's Bread Pudding***

INGREDIENTS:
2 eggs
1 ½ cups milk (375 ml)
1 teaspoon sugar (5 ml)
2 large slices of bread (or 4 small slices)
butter/margarine
¾ cup dried fruit (175 ml)
cinnamon
nutmeg

UTENSILS:
mixing bowl
fork
knife
set of measuring spoons
measuring cup
pie dish
larger baking dish

METHOD:
1. remove crusts from bread—butter bread
2. cut into neat squares or triangles
3. arrange in greased pie dish with the dried fruit
4. beat eggs with fork—add sugar and milk
5. pour over bread and fruit and allow to stand for 30 minutes
6. sprinkle top of pudding with a little cinnamon and nutmeg
7. place pie dish in baking dish, half filled with cold water
8. bake at 350°F (180°C) for one hour

The Story of Louis Braille

(a little boy shows how the disabled are able)

Many years ago there lived a little boy called Louis Braille. He lived with his family in a small village called Coupvray in France.

When Louis was three years old he had a dreadful accident. His eyes were terribly injured and he became blind. He would never see again.

"My poor little Louis," wept his mother. "What will become of him?"

In those days no one did very much to help blind children. They did not go to school, and when they grew up they often became beggars.

"We must not let this happen to Louis," said his father. "He must not grow up being too frightened to do anything. He must be allowed to live as other children do—to play and explore and wander freely."

"But he will fall over and injure himself," cried Louis' mother.

"Then we will pick him up and comfort him and let him try again," replied his father. "I will make him a long cane stick. That will help him to walk about safely."

So after that, Louis always went with his mother shopping, tap-tapping his way around the village.

"Do you want some bread, Mama?" he asked his mother one day as he stopped outside the baker's shop.

"How do you know we are at the baker's, my darling?" asked his mother in surprise.

"I can smell the fresh bread," laughed Louis.

Louis was learning to "see" through his ears too. Already he could tell his family and friends by the sounds of their footsteps.

Of course Louis was often lonely because he couldn't play some of the games the other children played, but he was a brave little boy and didn't tell anyone about his loneliness. Besides, he had a new friend, dear, kind Father Palluy, the village priest.

One day Father Palluy paid a visit to Monsieur Becheret, the schoolmaster.

"May I ask a favor of you, Monsieur Becheret?" asked Father Palluy. "Would you permit little Louis Braille to attend your school?"

Monsieur Becheret thought carefully, then he said, "Louis is most welcome to attend my school, Father. The company of the other children will be good for him. I will do my best to help him to learn."

How excited Louis was! He learned many things listening to Monsieur Becheret, but when it was time for the other children to have their reading lessons he felt very unhappy. If only he could read!

Then one day Father Palluy brought wonderful news to Louis' parents.

"A special school for blind children has opened in Paris," he told them.

"Paris is so far away," said Louis' mother, "but Louis must have his chance."

And so, at only ten years of age, Louis Braille left his family and went off all by himself in the stagecoach to Paris. At first he felt strange and alone, but then he heard a voice beside him say, "My name is Gabriel. I was new here once, and I know how scary it is. Would you like me to take you around?"

Louis and Gabriel were soon firm friends and Louis quickly got to know the other boys too. He was kept very busy. There were classes in maths and history and geography, and he learned to play his piano and the flute, and how to knit and how to do weaving.

Every afternoon the boys went for walks and explored Paris. Their teacher had a long rope and the little blind boys held onto the rope as they tap-tapped with their canes over their cobblestones of the Paris streets.

But best of all, Louis was learning to read! He learned to trace his fingers over letters which were raised up from the surface of the page. But it was a very hard way to learn to read. The letter "I" felt like a "T," and an "O" felt like a "Q."

Then one day a visitor arrived at the Institute (as Louis' school was called.) He was a soldier, a Captain Charles Barbier. The boys listened eagerly to what he had to say.

"Well, boys," said Captain Barbier, "I've worked out a way for my men to send messages in the dark, and I thought you might find it helpful. I call my method 'nightwriting.' "

Then the captain showed the little blind boys how to "read" his nightwriting. Each word was broken up into sounds. Each sound was made into a pattern of dots. The dots were pushed into thick paper by a stylus (rather like a blunt knitting needle). Then the paper was turned over and the soldiers used their fingers to "read" the dots.

"The trouble with nightwriting," said Louis to Gabriel, "it doesn't use capital letters or numbers. I've decided to work out a way to use raised dots to help blind children to read!"

And he was only twelve years old!

He set to work. He worked before breakfast and after dinner, on weekends and during holidays. Everywhere he went he took his stylus and his sheets of thick paper.

"I can't understand it," Louis said to Gabriel, "I can't get my patterns right. They're not simple enough. They take too long to read. It takes nearly one hundred dots to make just one word."

Then one night...three years later...

"Of course!" cried Louis to himself. "Of course! I won't use *sounds* to make up words. I'll use the *alphabet*!"

And that's what he did. He made a pattern of six dots. Then he numbered each dot.

1 o o 4
2 o o 5
3 o o 6

Then he pushed his stylus into Dot Number One.

● o
o o
o o

This was the pattern for A. Then

● o
● o B
o o

And so on, for the twenty-six letters of the alphabet.

"Would you mind trying my new patterns?" Louis asked the other boys shyly.

It worked! Their fingertips could read the dots easily!

"We can read! We can read!" they cried as they crowded around Louis.

Louis Braille had invented an alphabet that blind children could read with their fingers.

So when you hear someone say, "He's reading Braille," you can remember the story of the little blind boy, Louis Braille, who gave such a wonderful gift to the world.

And remember too...

It must be hard
To be deaf or blind
So think of others
And try to be kind.

TEST YOUR SENSES

When Louis Braille was a little boy he helped his mother with the cooking. How could Louis tell which *ingredients* he was using? He couldn't see them. Close your eyes and...

Smell and tell these ingredients: Cheese, cocoa, coffee, curry.

Touch and tell these ingredients: A hot dog, a potato, a boiled egg, a small bag of raisins.

Listen and tell these ingredients: Teacher shakes jars of rice, noodles, dried peas. Children observe and identify. Children close eyes, listen, identify.

How could Louis know which *utensils* he was using:

Touch and tell these utensils: Children close eyes, feel and identify: a spoon, an oven mitt, an egg cup, a cookie cutter.

Mother's Day

RECIPE: ***Mother's Day Yum Yums***

INGREDIENTS:
1 banana
⅓ cup dried fruits—raisins, apricots, dates, apples (75 ml)
⅔ cup rolled oats (150 ml)
coconut

UTENSILS:
mixing bowl
measuring cup
fork
knife
cutting board
large spoon

METHOD:
1. mash banana with fork
2. chop dried fruits
3. add fruits to the banana
4. add rolled oats
5. roll into balls
6. roll balls in coconut

Oh No! Not Again!

(a Mother's Day poem)

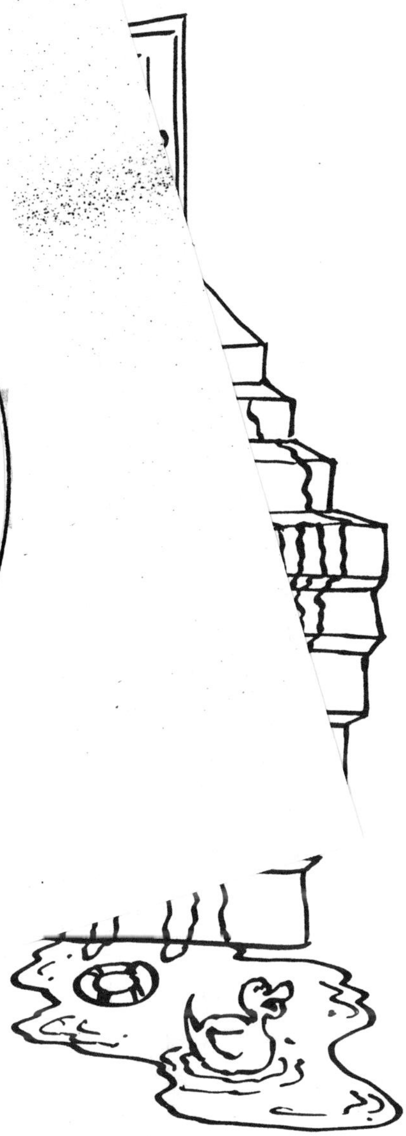

Mom, Mom
The dog's got out!
Oh no! Not again!

He's chasing the next-door
Chickens about!
Oh no! Not again!

Mom, Mom
There's a flood on the floor!
Oh no! Not again!

It's coming from under
The bathroom door!
Oh no! Not again!

Mom, Mom
The baby's sick!
Oh no! Not again!

She's covered in jam
Mom, come quick!

I'm coming! I'm coming!
Don't call me again!
I just have to wait
'Til I've counted to ten!

Conversation

Mothers have to "count to ten" quite often.

- Has *your* Mother ever had to "count to ten" because of something *you* have done? Tell the person next to you all about it.
- You might like to make some *Mother's Day Yum Yums.* When they are ready you could put them in a basket. Make a basket from
  - –an egg carton with the top removed, and the base decorated
  - –a strip of cardboard rolled and glued to a round base
  - –recycled yogurt or ice cream containers

Note: You could include your basket of Yum Yums with your pot of herbs and your leaf card. (See pp. 52 and 54 "Grow-Your-Own")

Father's Day

RECIPE: ***Father's Day Menu—Homemade Tomato Soup***

INGREDIENTS:

1 Tbsp. butter/margarine (15 ml)
1 teaspoon garlic powder (5 ml)
1 onion, chopped
1 medium carrot, peeled and diced
3 cups water (750 ml)
1 bouillon cube (chicken)
1 can crushed tomatoes
2 Tbsp. chopped basil (30 ml)
pepper and salt to taste

UTENSILS:

peeler
knives
large saucepan
set of measuring spoons
measuring cup
large mixing spoon

METHOD:

1. peel and chop vegetables
2. combine margarine/butter, onion, garlic, salt and pepper, and vegetables in saucepan
3. add water and bouillon cube
4. cover and cook over low heat for 20 minutes
5. add tomatoes and cook 10 minutes longer
6. add basil just before serving

RECIPE: **Father's Day Menu—Cheese Biscuits**

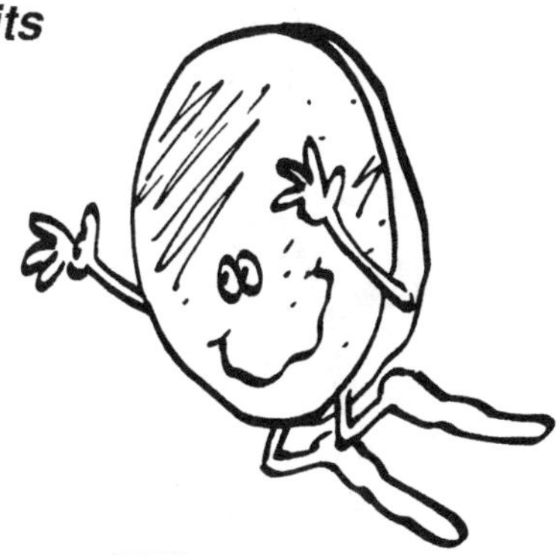

INGREDIENTS:

1 1/2 cups all purpose flour (375 ml)
3 teaspoons baking powder (15 ml)
1/4 teaspoon salt (1 ml)
1/3 cup butter/shortening (75 ml)
1/2 cup cheddar cheese, grated (125 ml)
1/2 cup buttermilk* (125 ml)
* you can make this from buttermilk powder

UTENSILS:

bowl
cheese grater
set of measuring spoons
measuring cup
cookie cutter
cookie sheet
pastry cutter or fork
wooden spoon
rolling pin

METHOD:

1. grate cheese
2. combine flour, baking powder, salt
3. cut in butter/shortening with pastry blender or fork until crumbly
4. add grated cheese
5. add buttermilk gradually
6. turn dough onto floured table and knead lightly
7. roll dough with floured rolling pin until 3/4 inch (3.5 cm) thick
8. cut with floured cookie cutter
9. place on ungreased cookie sheet
10. bake at 425°F (200°C) for 10–15 minutes (or until brown)

Father's Day at Michael and Jennifer's House

Michael and Jennifer were very pleased with their preparations for Father's Day. They asked Mommy if they could cook Father's Day lunch by themselves.

"What a good idea," she said. "What will you cook?"

"Tomato soup," said Michael.

"And cheese biscuits," said Jennifer. "Daddy loves tomato soup and cheese biscuits."

"And Christopher could make a play-dough cake," suggested Michael. (Christopher was their little baby brother.)

Michael and Jennifer were pleased with their Father's Day presents too. They'd saved up their pocket money and bought a sheet of bright yellow cardboard and some yellow paper. They cut up the cardboard into small cards about 8 cm x 4 cm. Then they printed fun things on the cards and drew pictures...like this...

Their baby brother Christopher had been watching them. He knew something special was happening. "Let's make a present for Christopher to give to Daddy," suggested Jennifer.

Michael agreed. He cut out a small square of cardboard and Jennifer put a crayon in Christopher's little hand and helped him draw a kiss on the cardboard square.

Then they decorated the yellow paper they had bought. They drew daddy pictures all over the paper...Daddy mowing the lawn, Daddy at the beach, Daddy cooking on the barbecue, Daddy reading them a story.

Last of all Michael and Jennifer wrapped up their Father's Day presents (and Christopher's) and hid them in special hiding places all over the house.

And as you can imagine their Daddy had a *super* Father's Day!

Christmas

RECIPE: **_Christmas Cake_**

INGREDIENTS:

½ cup butter/margarine (125 g)
½ cup brown sugar (125 ml)
¼ cup warm water (50 ml)
2 eggs
2 cups mixed dried fruit, washed (500 ml)
1 ½ cups all purpose flour (375 ml)
1 teaspoon baking powder (5 ml)
1 teaspoon cinnamon (5 ml)
½ teaspoon nutmeg (2 ml)
½ cup coconut (125 ml)
½ teaspoon almond extract (2 ml)

UTENSILS:

measuring cups
set of measuring spoons
mixing bowl
saucepan
greased and floured 9" cake pan (or 9" x 5" loaf pan)
knife
wooden spoon
hand beater (optional)

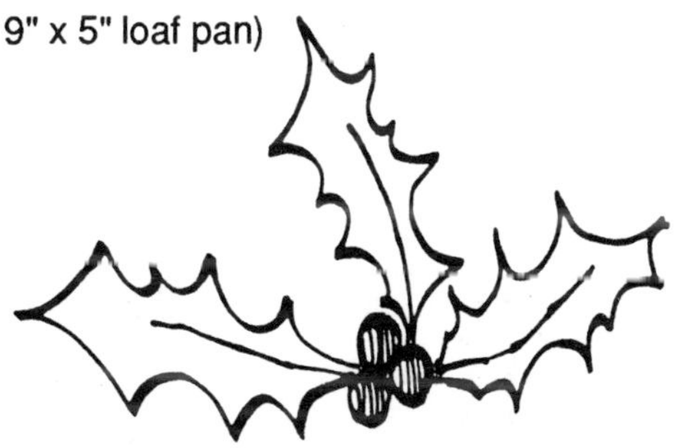

METHOD:

1. cream butter/margarine, and brown sugar
2. beat in eggs and almond flavoring
3. combine flour, baking powder, and spices
4. add water, and flour mixture to butter mixture
5. stir in fruit and mix well
6. spoon into greased and floured cake pan
7. bake at 300°F (150°C) for 2 hours

RECIPE: **_Christmas Crunchies_**

INGREDIENTS:
1 Tbsp. vegetable oil (15 ml)
2 eggs
2 cups Rice Krispies (500 ml)
1 cup dried fruits (250 ml)
1 cup coconut (250 ml)
⅔ cup brown sugar (150 ml)
1 teaspoon vanilla extract (5 ml)

UTENSILS:
mixing bowl
measuring cup
set of measuring spoons
saucepan
wooden spoon
greased pan
knife

METHOD:
1. add oil to saucepan
2. mix eggs, sugar, dried fruits, then add to oil
3. heat slowly over medium heat until smooth
4. add Rice Krispies, coconut, and vanilla extract and mix well
5. press into greased pan and refrigerate
6. cut into squares when cool

Baboushka

(a Christmas poem adapted from a Russian folk tale)

Baboushka lived
All alone
No one visited
Her little home
Deep in the woods
So she was surprised
When at her door
Three men arrived.

They were tired and cold
They had lost their way
They asked Baboushka
If they could stay
They wouldn't stop long
They were seeking a Child
"Come in," she said
"And rest a while."

She gave them soup
And cheese and bread
And they told her about
A star which led
Them on their journey
To find the Child
The little baby
Meek and mild.

They showed her the gifts
They were taking to Him
They were precious gifts
Fit for a king
Then, thanking her
They went away
To find the star
To show them the way.

Baboushka decided
To follow them
She took the road
To Bethlehem
Before she left
She packed some toys
To give to the dear
Little baby boy.

A knitted ball
A colored stone
A bright little feather
A new pine cone
Then off she went
She travelled far
But she could not find
The guiding star.

One day as she wandered
All alone
She found some children
On their own
They were hungry and lost
They were orphans you see
They had no parents
Or family.

She had no money
To buy them food
Or shelter or firewood
Or blankets or shoes
But she gave them the toys
She'd brought for the Child
They took them shyly
And thanked her with smiles.

Baboushka never
Found the star
Though she searched and searched
And travelled far
But wherever she went
She gave a toy
To every poor
Little girl and boy.

Baboushka never
Saw the Child
She's searching still
Though she's old and tired
But hundreds of children
Became her friends
And that is how
Her story ends.

Christmas Greetings

France	Joyeux Noel
Germany	Froehliche Weihnachten
Greece	Kala Christougena
Italy	Bono Natale
Japan	Meri Kurisumasu
Norway	Glendalig Jul
Wales	Nadolig Llawen
Denmark	Glaedelig Jul
Holland	Zalig Kerstfeast
Poland	Boze Narodzeme
Canada	Merry Christmas!

Learn how to pronounce these Christmas greetings.

Make a class book of Christmas thoughts.

CHRISTMAS CUSTOMS

Christmas is celebrated in different ways in different countries.
• Does *your* family celebrate Christmas? How?
I know a Grandfather who goes around saying "Ho! Ho! Ho!" all the time. He *loves* Christmas.

CHRISTMAS GIFTS

Every Christmas the people of Oslo, Norway, send the people of London, England, a 60-foot (20-meter) Christmas tree to commemorate World War links between Norway and England.

This giant Christmas tree can be seen in Trafalgar Square every Christmas. It is possibly the world's largest Christmas tree.

Christmas is a time for sharing and caring.

- What happens to people who are ill in hospitals at Christmas?
- What happens to people who do not have families or people who cannot afford special meals or gifts at Christmas?
- How are these people helped?
- Perhaps your class could help them too!